Alexander Geddes

A Letter to the Right Reverend the Lord Bishop of London

Containing queries, doubts and difficulties, relative to a vernacular version of the Holy Scriptures. Being an appendix to A prospectus of a new translation of the Bible from a corrected text

Alexander Geddes

A Letter to the Right Reverend the Lord Bishop of London
Containing queries, doubts and difficulties, relative to a vernacular version of the Holy Scriptures. Being an appendix to A prospectus of a new translation of the Bible from a corrected text

ISBN/EAN: 9783337285746

Printed in Europe, USA, Canada, Australia, Japan

Cover: Foto ©Lupo / pixelio.de

More available books at **www.hansebooks.com**

A LETTER

TO THE RIGHT REVEREND

THE LORD BISHOP OF LONDON:

CONTAINING

QUERIES, DOUBTS AND DIFFICULTIES, RELATIVE TO A
VERNACULAR VERSION OF THE HOLY SCRIPTURES.

BEING AN

APPENDIX

TO A PROSPECTUS OF A NEW TRANSLATION OF THE BIBLE,
FROM A CORRECTED TEXT OF THE ORIGINALS, &c.

BY

THE REVEREND ALEXANDER GEDDES, L.L.D.

LONDON:

PRINTED BY J. DAVIS,
FOR ROBERT FAULDER, NEW BOND-STREET.
M,DCC,LXXXVII.

A LETTER, &c.

MY LORD,

WHEN I firſt ſat down to tranſlate the Hebrew Scriptures, I knew I was undertaking a moſt arduous taſk; but, I confeſs, I was not ſufficiently aware of all the difficulties that have ſince occurred. If I had, I ſhould then, perhaps, have prudently declined an enterprize, which I cannot, without puſillanimity, now relinquiſh.

However, as new obſtacles are daily preſenting themſelves, and doubts and perplexities ſeem to multiply in proportion as I proceed, I have reduced a part of theſe into a ſet of Queries, which I beg leave to lay before your Lordſhip, as the perſon in the kingdom the moſt likely to give me a ſatisfactory ſolution of them.

The firſt queſtion that naturally offers is, how far the ſtile and phraſeology of our laſt Engliſh Verſion ought to be adopted or rejected, in a new tranſlation? But to form a juſt idea of this general queſtion, it will be proper to divide it into different heads.

In the firſt place, then, I think it will be by all agreed, that ſuch ſingle words or whole phraſes, in the old verſion, as are become entirely obſolete, or are of an ambiguous meaning, or border on plebeian triteneſs, ought, by a new tranſlator, to be rejected; and others ſubſtituted in their place, more agreeable to the preſent uſage, leſs liable to miſconſtruction, and further removed from vulgarity. But is the ſame liberty to be taken with other words and phraſes, which, though obſolete in common uſe, are ſtill intelligible to one acquainted with the Scripture ſtile, and have in reality nothing in them to debaſe its dignity?

For example, would you, with ſome faſtidious moderns, reject ſuch words as *ambuſhment, heritage, meet, wroth, banquet, banner, bereave, bewail, pourtray, diſcomfit, marvel, obeiſance, progenitors,* and a number of ſimilar terms throughout the Bible? Or would you occaſionally uſe them for the ſake of variety, energy, or euphony? For my part I am inclined to think, and have elſewhere hinted, that we ſhould not only retain ſuch old words as are ſtill, though rarely uſed; but even revive many that have gradually gone into difuſe; if they be equally analogical, and at the ſame time more ſignificant and harmonious than thoſe that cuſtom has introduced in their room.

With regard to whole phrafes, it is much harder to form a decided opinion. They are generally Hebraifms, which have been gradually incorporated into our language by the different tranflators of the Bible, from a laudable defign of reprefenting, as exactly as poffible, the air of the originals; and, though many of them are extremely abhorrent from the Englifh idiom, yet long cuftom and the fanction of religion have made them familiar to our ear; however indiftinctly they may be feized by our underftanding—Are fuch to be retained by a new tranflator? or mollified and modernized into equivalent terms?

It will poffibly be faid: " A diftinction fhould be made. Some " Hebraifms are fo contrary to our modes of phrafing, that they " cannot be retained without great obfcurity; whilft others, though " fomewhat uncouth, are yet intelligible, or may be eafily made fo " by a note. The latter fhould, the former fhould not be adopted " in a vernacular tranflation."

But this feems, by far, too vague an anfwer. What may appear fufficiently clear to one, may feem obfcure to another; and in a book, that is read by all, it is not enough that the phrafe be intelligible to a few perfons only; it fhould be as generally fo as poffible. It is granted by the greateft fticklers for verbal tranflation, that the phrafeology of the original ought to be abandoned for abfolute perfpicuity: why not, then, for a greater degree of it? efpecially where there is no danger of miftaking the meaning by fuch a licence——This deferves a more attentive confideration.

I had said in my PROSPECTUS, that there is, in our laſt national Verſion, a blameable want of uniformity in the mode of tranſlating. It has been hinted to me, that I ought to have produced inſtances, which I now do the more willingly, becauſe it gives me an opportunity of diſcuſſing the queſtion under conſideration, and others connected with it.

When I rank, among the faults of a tranſlation, a want of uniformity in the mode of rendering, I do not mean that a tranſlator is never to diverſify his ſtile, or vary his expreſſions. The contrary I have laid down as one of the qualities of a good tranſlation. But ſtill, that diverſity ſhould be regulated by ſome uniform and conſiſtent principle, from which he ſhould never deviate, without the moſt cogent reaſons.

There are many words, as well as ſentences, in the Bible, which admit, and often require a different rendering; becauſe they have a different meaning in the original. But there are, likewiſe, many words and ſentences, that either always, or at leaſt in ſimilar circumſtances, have the ſame preciſe meaning; and, conſequently, ſhould always be rendered in the ſame, or nearly the ſame terms; and this only is the uniformity which I contend for. I will now give examples, both of words and ſentences, in which this uniformity has not been obſerved by our laſt tranſlators.

Firſt, of words——And, here, I make not much account of ſuch variations as may poſſibly be deemed ſynonimous. He would be a ſuperci-

supercilious critick, I think, who should blame our translators for using indiscriminately *branch* or *bough*; *fountain* or *spring*; *bird* or *fowl*; *faint* or *weary*; *dwelling-place* or *habitation*; *wrathful* or *furious*; *pot, pan* or *cauldron*; *tent, tabernacle* or *pavilion*; *vale, valley* or *dale*; *target, shield* or *buckler*; *mitre, hood* or *diadem*; *maid, maiden, damsel* or *young-woman*; to *beat-down, break-down, throw-down, destroy* or *overthrow*; to *pluck-up, pluck-out, root-up* or *root-out*; to *wail*, to *mourn* or *to lament*, &c. Although, perhaps, strictly speaking, it would be better to make some appropriate distinction in the use of almost every one of these and such terms.* But when we find איל rendered in one place a *lintel*, in another a *post*; ארבה now a *locust*, and now a *grass-hopper*; לענה *wormwood* and *hemlock*; קמוש nettles

* The copiousness of a language is somewhat like a superabundance of wealth; there are few who know how to make a good use of either; and he only who is blest with superlative taste and judgment will be kept, in both cases, from manifold abuses. To such a degree has the Lexicon of our language been gradually enriched, that it is often more difficult to select terms, than to find them; and a proper choice is one of the principal characters of good writing. For this the Greek authors are peculiarly remarkable. Although the storehouse from which they drew was inexhaustible, yet they seldom drew from it at random. Almost every term, in their best compositions, has a discriminating character, which is very rarely confounded with any other, however approximating. But, in Greece, no one wrote, who had not made a long and laborious study of the Greek tongue; whereas, in England, almost every one is a writer; and almost every one gives a currency to some new impropriety. Since your Lordship's little book appeared, and since Johnson wrote his Dictionary, grammatical precision has been more generally aimed at, than before; but not much attention, I fear, has been given to the sort of propriety, of which I am speaking; although that, with a little more variety and harmony in the arrangement of sentences, and a more rational application of our indeclinable particles, is all that our language seems to want of the perfection, of which it is susceptible.

nettles and *thorns*; ראיש *hemlock* and *gall*; יענה an *owl* and an *ostrich*; שש *linen* and *silk*; קאת the *cormorant* and the *pelican*; שאל *hell* and the *grave*, &c. we cannot possibly but disapprove of such incongruity in rendering; and point it out as a fault to be studiously guarded against by every translator.

All this appears to be indisputable. But there are words, in the rendering of which, our translators took a latitude, which, though it is by no means so exceptionable as the former, seems yet to have a certain want of uniformity in it, that in some measure misrepresents the text; and may actually mislead the reader. For what reader would imagine that *law, statute, decree, ordinance* were all terms so perfectly synonimous, as to be expressed by one Hebrew word? Yet חק is found rendered by all those terms. A *coat of mail*, a *habergeon*, a *breast-plate* and a *brigandine* all imply a piece of defensive armour of much the same nature; yet I hardly think that any one would expect to see them all represented in the Original by the single word שרין. Will it appear any more likely that מצר or מצרה is translated with equal propriety, a *fort*, a *hold*, a *strong hold*, a *castle*, a *bulwark*, a *munition?* The three first are more general terms, and may denote any *strong place*, whether so by nature or art; but the three last give us the idea of manual fortification. In all such cases it would, in my apprehension, be more proper to stick to one term, which term should be the most distinctive and expressive that could be found.

We

We should not, perhaps, even approve of translating the same Hebrew words by different English ones, though of nearly the same import; when these, in common acceptation, have at least a sensible difference of meaning in magnitude, intensity, degree or relation. Can a *flood*, a *river*, and a *brook* be equally proper renderings of יאר? or a *town* and a *village* of בת? *vessels, furniture, stuff, instruments, weapons, armour, artillery* of כלי?* a *castle* and a *palace* of טיר? *coal* and *hot coal* of גחל? *concubine* and *paramour* of פלגש? *nephew* and *grandson* of נכד? *inchanters, observers of times* and *sooth-sayers* of ענן? Those who wish to see more of this diversity, may consult Taylor's Concordance under the words עלה. עלם. פה. פנה. יתן. נפש. יכף. יום. שוב. קרא. קום. קול.

Nay further, I am not sure but we should uniformly translate the same Hebrew word by the same English word; unless the former have a multifarious meaning; or perspicuity or embellishment require to vary the latter. If *tabret* be a good rendering of תך why translate it also *timbrel?* What need is there for translating כימה in one place the *Pleiades*, and in another the *seven stars?* Why is שמים sometimes rendered *heaven*, sometimes *the heaven*, some-

---

* To shew how little attentive our translators were to uniformity in rendering the same word even in the very same construction and sense, I shall here give a remarkable instance. Exod. xxx. ver. 27, 28. We have the word כליו three times translated " his vessels:" yet in the very next chapter, ver. 8, 9. we find the same word, not only in the same construction, but relatively to the same things, rendered three times " his furniture." One can hardly suppose that these two chapters were translated by the same person.

times *the heavens,* and sometimes the *air?* Why גוים—*nations, gentiles* and *heathen?* Why אמה a *maid,* a *bond-woman,* a *bond-maid,* a *hand-maid,* a *maid-servant?* Why תבנית a *pattern,* a *figure,* a *likeness,* a *form,* a *similitude?* Why גוע *to die, to perish, to give* and *yield up the ghost?* Why חשה to *be silent,* to *keep silence,* to *hold one's peace,* to *hold one's tongue?* Any of thefe refpective terms, well-chofen at firft, would furely be more uniform, and for the moft part more proper.

What has been faid with regard to the inconfiftency and incongruity of rendering the fame Hebrew word, in the fame circumftances, by different vernacular terms; is equally applicable to the rendering of different Hebrew words by the fame term. If I have once ufed the word tabernacle to exprefs משכן and tent to exprefs אהל; I will uniformly do fo throughout—nor will I confound either with בית. It is hardly poffible that אכל. בזז. חתף. טרף. לקח. and שלל can all be equally well tranflated by one word "prey." In fact, moft of the Hebrew terms have peculiar ideas annexed to them, that require a diverfity in rendering them.*

It often happens, indeed, that this diverfity cannot be attained, becaufe the language into which we tranflate has not fuch a number

---

* The want of this diftinction has made our tranflators put in the mouth of Cain, what he could not fay, nor mean—"Behold thou driveft me this day from the face of the earth!" Q. Whither then was he driven? Was not the land of Nod on the face of the earth? The word is אדמה not ארץ and means the fpot he was then on; ιχ ταυτη τη γη ειπων, as S. Chryfoftome well expreffes it.

of difcriminating terms as would be neceffary to exprefs it (not to mention that the etymon of the original word is often dubious, and the diftinction fometimes, perhaps, imaginary); but then as far as its terms go, they are to be employed, and appropriated, as nearly as poffible, to the ideas meant to be conveyed by them. See fome very fenfible obfervations on this fubject in Pilkington's Remarks, Sect. xxv.

Diverfity in rendering whole fentences, or parts of fentences, is not lefs common with our tranflators, than in rendering fingle words; and is frequently lefs excufable. This is, no doubt, that " want of " identity of phrafing" which the prefacers, in fome fort, apologize for; and which is chiefly obfervable in their tranflation of Hebraifms; which are the principal object of our prefent difcuffion.

Now in rendering thefe, they feem to have been guided by no uniform principle, nor even by any rules of grammatical analogy: for they have not only obferved no uniformity in rendering fimilar fentences, but have often admitted a ftrange variety in rendering the fame fentences. *To lift up one's feet* for " *to remove*" is certainly not a more harfh idiotifm than *to lift up one's eyes* for " *to look up.*" Nay the word *lift*, in ftrict propriety, is more literally applicable to the feet than to the eyes: yet our tranflators every where retain the laft Hebraifm; never the firft. I am aware it will be faid, that the firft feems more uncouth to our ears than the laft; but I am perfuaded it was not more uncouth, when the laft was firft adopted; and that if they had also adopted the first, it would now be as familiar to us as the other.* But the Latin version seems to have determined them; which has *elevavit oculos,* but not *elevavit pedes.* Yet the Greek has retained the last Hebraism: Genesis xxix. 1. Και εξαρας Ιακωβ τες ποδας.

In like manner, " to deliver one's self from the eyes of another" for " to escape from one," is not more abhorrent from our idiom than " to hide one's eyes from another" for " to connive at him:" yet in the former case, our translators rejected the Hebraism. 2 Sam. xx. 6. but retained it in the latter. Levit. xx. 4.

To do what is *good* in one's eyes, is a Hebraism which our translators have generally rendered by, doing what *pleaseth* or *liketh* one. Thus Gen. xvi. 6. " Behold thy maid is in thy hand; do to her " as it pleaseth thee." And Esther viii. 8. " Write ye also to the " Jews, as it liketh you." But in a phrase exactly similar, Jud. xvii. 6. they translate, " Every one did that which was right in " his own eyes." Again, Gen. xli. 37. " And the thing was good " in the eyes of Pharoah." But Num. xi. 10. they have not translated " It was also evil in the eyes of Moses," but " Moses was also " displeased."

* It is observable that the most of our former translators retained the Hebraism: " Jacob lyfte up hys fete and wente, &c." Tyndal—And so Matthews, Cranmer—Bish. Gen. and even Purver. Luther too has " her hub Jacob seine fuesse auff"—And the Dutch " hief Jacob sijne voeten op." Diodati, with his usual elegance, gave the phrase another term, but still renders the word רגל by *feet* " *Se messe in camino a* " *piedi.*" The Genevans translated as we do. " *Se mit en chemin.*"

But there are no phrases, in the rendering of which they have shewn more variety than in those of which the words בן and איש make a part. The first of these, which primarily signifies a *son*, and secondarily a descendant of any kind; has, in the oriental dialects, a much wider acceptation; and is applied not only to the offspring of the brute creation, but also to productions of every sort; and what is still more catachrestical, even to consequential or concomitant relations: So that an *arrow* is called *the son of the bow*; *the morning star*, *the son of the morning*; *threshed-out corn*, *the son of the floor*; and *anointed persons*, the sons of oil.

Now our translators have, in rendering such phrases, for the most part softened the Hebraism; but after no uniform manner. *Sons of Belial* בני בליעל is surely not more intelligible to an English reader than *Sons of oil*; and much less so than *Sons of valour, sons of righteousness, sons of iniquity*; yet, while they retain the first Hebraism with all its original harshness, and partly in its original form;* they mollify the three last into *valiant men, righteous men, wicked men*.

---

* Even here they are not consistent. For if once they admitted the word *Belial*, they should have retained it throughout; and said *a thing of Belial, a heart of Belial, a witness of Belial, the floods of Belial:* which, however, they render *an evil disease, a wicked heart, an ungodly witness, the floods of ungodliness.* Nay they have, once or twice, translated איש בליעל and אדם בליעל *a wicked man.* At any rate, if such phrases were not good English in the Old Testament; how came they to adopt them in the New? For there we meet with " The child of hell, the children of light, the children of wrath, the " son of perdition, &c."

The same inconsistency holds with regard to אִישׁ in a similar construction. If they could, without hurting the English idiom, translate *a man of war*, *a man of understanding*, *a man of sorrows*, *a man of strife*, *a man of wicked devices*, *the man of thy right hand*; why not also *a man of peace*, *a man of truth*, *a man of violence*, *a man of iniquity?*

Not only in similar phrases, did our translators break the rules of uniformity; they often violated them in rendering the same phrase, and that, sometimes, in the same chapter. " How old art thou?" says Pharoah to Jacob, Gen. xlvii. 8. instead of " How many are " the days of thy years?" But in Jacob's answer, verse 9. " The " days of the years of my pilgrimage are &c." In ver. 28. they again drop the Hebraism, and translate " so the whole age of " Jacob ;" for " all the days of the years of Jacob."

To be in one's hand, is a Hebraism that often signifies *to be in one's power*, and so our translators rendered it, Job i. 12. " All that he " hath is in thy power :" but Gen. xvi. 6. they retain the Hebraism, " Behold thy maid is in thy hand."

To lift up one's hand is *to swear*; and so we find it rendered, Exod. vi. 8. " Which I did swear to give." Num. xiv. 30. " Which I " sware to make you dwell therein." Nehem. ix. 15. " Which " thou hadst sworn to give them." But Gen. xiv. 22. " I have " lift up my hand to the Lord"—and Deuter. xxxii. 40. " I lift
" up

" up my hand to Heaven." And Ezek. xx. 5. " In the day when
" I chofe Ifrael, and lifted up mine hand unto the feed of the houfe
" of Jacob." Many more fuch inftances may be found under the
word יד. *

The fame variety appears in the rendering of איש מלחמה *a man
of war*. Thus Exod. xv. 3. " The Lord is a man of war:" but
Pfalm xxiv. 8. " The Lord mighty in battle." Again, Num.
xxxi. 49. " Thy fervants have taken the fum of the men of war:"
but in the fame chapter, ver. 27. " Them that took the war upon
" them." The LXX. generally rendered the words by πολεμιϛης;
and our tranflators have ufed *warrior* and *warriors* in the fame fenfe,
on fimilar occafions. 1 Kings xii. 21. " Fourfcore thoufand men
" which were warriors" עשה מלחמה; which 2 Chron. xxvi. 11.
they render " fighting men."

" To be *wife* or *right* in one's own eyes," is a Hebraifm perfectly
" intelligible in any other language, and is in ours not unfrequently
ufed in common fpeech. Yet, even in rendering this phrafe, our
tranflators varied. Thus Prov. xiii. 7. " Be not wife in thine own
" eyes." Prov. xii. 15. " The way of a fool is right in his own
" eyes." But Prov. xxvi. 5. " Anfwer not a fool according to his folly,
" left he be wife in his own conceit." And xxviii. 11. " The rich
" man is wife in his own conceit."

* What makes a deviation from the Hebraifm here more neceffary is, becaufe " to lift
" up one's hand" fignifies alfo *to rebel*, and fometimes to *chaftife*.

In

In Exod. iv. 15. they tranſlate וְשַׂמְתָּ אֶת הַדְּבָרִים בְּפִיו, " Thou " ſhalt put words in his mouth." But Ezra viii. 17. they render וָאָשִׂימָה בְּפִיהֶם דְּבָרִים לְדַבֵּר, " I told them what they ſhould " ſay." Should not the Hebraiſm have been retained in both places; or in neither?

In Numb. viii. 7. הֶעֱבִירוּ תַעַר עַל כָּל בְּשָׂרָם are rendered, equivalently " Let them ſhave all their fleſh;" but Ezek. v. 1. the Hebraiſm is retained; " Let a razor paſs on thy head."

In fine, our tranſlators appear to have, not ſeldom, changed the Hebraiſm, without neceſſity, and when it is equally plain, and as good Engliſh as the ſubſtituted phraſe. " Come ye after me" is as intelligible as " follow me"—" To cut off the ends or extremities of a " country" is as intelligible, and it ſhould ſeem leſs vulgar than " to " cut a country ſhort." See 2 Kings vi. 19. and x. 23. So Prov. iv. 26. " Ponder the path of thy feet, and let all thy ways be " eſtabliſhed." The Hebraiſm of the laſt part of this ſentence, " and " all thy ways ſhall be ordered aright," which is the marginal rendering, is no leſs clear and expreſſive than what has been adopted in its ſtead. Again, Prov. vi. 16. " Six *things* doth the Lord hate; yea, " ſeven are an abomination to him." I miſtake if it would not have been better to retain the Hebraiſm; " Yea, ſeven are the " abomination of his ſoul." Prov. xxvi. 20. the Hebrew has, " Without wood the fire goeth out," which our tranſlators, with the

help

help of Italics, paraphrase thus: " Where no wood *is*, *there* the fire
" goeth out," which, compared with the other, appears languid and
drawling. Psalm xci. 16. " With long life will I satisfy him."
The Hebraism, " with length of days, &c," seems not only as clear,
but more energetic and poetical.

Enough has been said to shew, that our translators were not guided
by any uniform rule in rendering the Hebraisms of the Bible.—But
are there then no rules to be guided by? No fixt and certain boundaries to be prescribed to a translator? Or may he, at random and
in an arbitrary manner, either follow the Hebraism, or abandon it? I
scarcely think, that this will be allowed by any rational Philologist.
I will, therefore, venture to lay down some general Canons, by
which I myself have been directed; and of which I wish to obtain
your Lordship's and the public's approbation.

I CANON.

All Hebraisms that are sufficiently clear to exclude ambiguity; and
either were from the beginning, or are become by long usage, intelligible to every class of readers; and, at the same time, have
nothing in them that offends against the laws of grammar and good
writing, should universally be retained: but those that are obscure,
equivocal, uncouth and ungrammatical should as universally be
rejected.

II CANON.

II CANON.

In rendering the poetical and sentential parts of Scripture, bolder Hebraisms are allowable, than in the historical and legislative parts.

III CANON.

Whatever Hebraism has been once adopted, or Anglicism substituted, should, in the same sort of stile, and in circumstances exactly similar, be uniformly and universally retained.

As to the particular application of these canons, it must, I fear, be left to the judgment and taste of the translator. For whatever lights he may borrow from the observations of others, still it must ultimately rest with himself, how far he is to be directed by them; or on what occasions he is to prefer them to his own.

Another question, starting out of the former, is; Should the Hebraisms, that are not admitted into the text, be retained, at least, in the margin?

Bishop Newcome is decidedly of opinion that they should; and has, accordingly, crowded the margin of his Version of the minor Prophets with more Hebraisms than are even in our common translation. His reason is: "That the genius of the original "language will, by that means, be shewn; and the reader unskilled "in them will be best enabled to interpret for himself." Your Lordship seems to be of a different opinion, if we may judge

from

from your Ifaiah; and I find that many learned perfons, whom I have occafionally confulted on the point, agree with you.

Indeed, I can fee little advantage, that either the learned or unlearned can derive from fuch marginal renderings. Thofe who are fkilled in the languages have no need of them; and thofe who are unfkilled can only view them as fo many ftrange modes of expreffion; which muft give them no favourable idea of the oriental ftile. This, I know it from experience, is the idea which the common people entertain of them. They look upon them as fo many obftacles on the way fide, that retard their journey; and they generally prefer Bibles that have them not. To what purpofe then perplex them with fo unneceffary an adjunct; which, at every other verfe, draws their attention from a clear *Text* to an obfcure Comment? For in that light every thing in the margin is by them confidered.

The fole clafs of readers, to whom they can be of any fervice, is that of Biblical Students, who wifh to make the Englifh tranflation a fort of guide to the grammatical knowledge of the originals, without the trouble of learning Hebrew Grammar. But thefe, I prefume, are few in number, and have, befides, if they underftand Latin, a much better director in Arias Montanus.

There are only two cafes, in which I would admit marginal renderings. The firft is, when the tranflator doubts whether he have given the true meaning of the original in the text. Then he is not only sufficiently authorized, but obliged, I think, in justice, to give either a different English rendering of equal probability, or a literal version of the Hebraism. The second is, when the meaning or force of the text cannot well be perceived without the interpretation of some proper name or emblematical term; in which case, if the English interpretation be admitted into the text, the Hebrew word should be referred to in the margin; and so *vice versa*. Though perhaps it would be still better to include the rejected term in a parenthesis, immediately after the admitted one.

I come now to another question. Beside such idiotisms as I have already mentioned, there is in every language a number of expletive and redundant words, which originating in colloquial dialect, no where grammatical, too often retain their place in the most refined and cultivated languages; the first writers not daring to lay them aside, and their example giving them a sanction among those who write after them. How many such are there not in English, which we have not yet had the courage to explode?

In translating a Greek or Latin work into any modern language, or a work of one modern language into another, we never think it necessary to express those idiomatical redundancies; nay, for the honour of our author, we avoid expressing them as much as possible. But a different procedure has generally been observed with regard to the Hebrew Scriptures. Not only to deviate from their meaning; but, likewise, from their form, construction, anomalies, tautologies, ellipsises,

fifes, pleonafms, enallagès, hypallagés—nay, from the very blunders of their various tranfcribers, was long accounted a kind of audacious facrilege.

Hence, no doubt, it is that fo many of them have been retained in moft modern tranflations; in direct oppofition to grammar and logic; and often to the great detriment of the text, and obfcurity of the verfion. This unjuft and ill-grounded prejudice is, among the learned, no more a predominant one: and the tranflator of the Bible, if he be but a faithful interpreter, may now, without the imputation of impiety, follow that mode of tranflation which he moft approves of; and which is the moft likely to convey to the reader the genuine fpirit, not the bare and barren letter, of his originals.

Under the fhelter of this privilege, may I here prefume to point out fuch Hebrew expletives and pleonafms, as I think may be, with advantage, fuppreffed in an Englifh tranflation.

In the firft place, the copulative ו which admits, and has in every tranflation received, a great number of various acceptations*, might frequently with great propriety be omitted altogether; and has often been omitted by the beft interpreters, both ancient and modern.

I would

---

* It is indeed the general link of fentences; and ferves not only for all thofe particles which we call conjunctions; but alfo for many adverbs and prepofitions, and even pronouns. Noldius gives it above feventy different meanings: but his diftinctions are often nice; and I think they are all reducible to the following thirty: *And, or, nor, nay, with, fo, alfo, thus, if, although, becaufe, that, for, but, yet, fince, indeed, tells,*

I would, alſo, extend this licence to the ſame letter in combination with יהי; though here again I have the misfortune to have the whole weight of Biſhop Newcome's authority in the oppoſite ſcale.

who, when, then, now, afterwards, again, whilſt, meanwhile, therefore, wherefore, namely, nevertheleſs, moreover. Of theſe the moſt generally uſed, and perhaps the only neceſſary, are *and, again, when, for, but, that, if, although, with.* This laſt is, in reality, no leſs a copulative than *and*; and a more general uſe of it would give perſpicuity, energy and preciſion to many paſſages of Holy Writ, which from the conſtant uſe of *and* and *and*, are amphibologous, languid, indiſcriminate and ungrammatical. We have a remarkable inſtance in the three firſt verſes of Geneſis. In theſe, three diſtinct ideas are preſented——The original creation of our material world—its chaotic primordial ſtate—and the important change that took place at the period of the ſix days creation. It is, moreover, evident from the form and arrangement of the Hebrew words, that ſuch a diſtinction was meant by the writer. For חיש being without a verb, and רוח being joined to a participle, are naturally and ſtrictly connected with what immediately goes before; but with what follows only by contraſt. It is therefore impoſſible that the ן can be equally well rendered by " and," through the whole of the three verſes. Let us ſee: " In the beginning God created the Heavens AND the " earth, AND the earth was without form AND void, AND darkneſs was upon the face " of the deep, AND the ſpirit of God moved upon the face of the waters: AND God ſaid, " Let there be light, AND there was light." How heavy, how monotonous, how like to the tale of a peaſant is this narrative! But to do juſtice to the author of the Pentateuch, who, as Longinus ſays, was certainly no mean writer, let us combine the above paſſage as ſenſe and conſtruction point out; and the three forementioned diſtinct ideas will immediately appear conſpicuous. In the beginning God created (or had created) the Heavens AND the earth. The earth was YET a diſmal waſte, WITH darkneſs on the face of the deep; AND a mighty wind (ſee p. 49,) moving upon the ſurface of the waters: WHEN God ſaid, " Let there be light;" AND light there was. Here there are only two common variations in rendering, and no need of an italic ſupplement to connect the ſenſe; and yet—But I ſhall leave the intelligent reader to make the compariſon of theſe two modes of tranſlating; and only obſerve that the firſt variation of the copulative is juſtified by the Greek tranſlation, and by the Vulgate ἡ δὲ γη —*Terra* AUTEM: and that the connection of רוח אלהים with what precedes is implied by their employing the imperfect time ἐπιφέρετο—*ferebatur.*

He

He thinks your Lordſhip's tranſlation of Iſaiah xxxviii. 1. defective; becauſe you have omitted " Now it came to paſs." But if one were to aſk his Lordſhip, whether he think that the Prophet, if he had written in Engliſh, would have expreſſed himſelf in that manner? I am perſuaded he would anſwer in the negative. If ſo, it is then evidently a Hebrew pleonaſm, that ſhould not be rendered in Engliſh. At any rate, it ſhould not be rendered, " Now it came to paſs," which never could have entered into the head of an Engliſh tranſlator, but for the Greek εγενετο and the Latin *factum eſt*. If it were at all to be tranſlated, in the paſſage above mentioned and other ſimilar paſſages, why not " It was (or it happened) in the four-" teenth year of King Hezekiah, that &c."

With regard to the word לאמר for the omiſſion of which your Lordſhip is alſo blamed, in the ſame paſſage (Pref. to the Minor Prophets, p. xix.) I think it may be ſometimes tranſlated with propriety; and ſometimes left untranſlated. When the word דבר precedes, I would for the moſt part tranſlate it; but when it is preceded by אמר I would not tranſlate it; unleſs that אמר could be conveniently rendered *ſpoke*, and not *ſaid*.* There is only one caſe that, to me, preſents a difficulty. It is, when לאמר follows a meſ-
ſage.

* The ſecond לאמר was ſometimes neglected even by the Oriental tranſlators, though, in their dialects, it was idiomatical. Thus SYRIAC, Joſhua i. 1. renders the Hebr. ויאמר יהוה לאמר by only אמר מריא; and ſo in other places—The Greeks

fage. " It was told him, *faying*—word was brought to him, *faying*." Here the rules of Englifh Grammar are manifeftly violated; and yet I cannot fee how they can be adhered to, without deviating from the ftile and manner of the originals, and almoft always diminifhing their fimplicity. Should we, for the fake of Grammar, even at thefe rifks, adopt the indirect mode of expreffing the meffage, inftead of the direct? Or fhould we fay, " This word, this " meffage was brought to David?" Or, in fine, fhould we retain the prefent verfion, ungrammatical as it is, as being the leaft of the three evils?

The words לי. לך. לו. and their refpective plurals are alfo mere expletives, that may be frequently omitted in a tranflation, to which they are not only not neceffary, but often give a vulgar air. " Build me an altar—Get thee up—Take to thee a wife—Come " curfe me Jacob—Affemble me the men of Judah—Take thou " alfo unto thee—Jacob took to him rods of green poplar." In thefe and all fuch phrafes the pronoun, it fhould feem, would be better omitted. Nay, our tranflators themfelves have fometimes

Greeks and Jerom made the repetition lefs difgufting by varying their words—ειπε, λεγων—*locutus eft, dicens.* In which they have been generally imitated by modern tranflators: and this accords perfectly with the exceptional diftinction I have made; for "he fpoke, faying;" or " he fpoke, and faid" has no air of tautology any more than דבר לאמר—It is remarkable that, although this phrafe is frequent in the Hebrew writings, we never find אמר לדבר.

omitted

omitted it, as Ezek. xii. 5. " Dig thou" for " dig thou thee;" and verse 7. " I digged" instead of " I digged me."*

The personal pronouns הוא and היא seem redundant in such phrases as these: " The woman, whom thou gavest to be with me, "*she* gave me of the tree——And Debora, a Prophetess, the wife " of Lapidoth, *she* judged Israel at that time—Now Hannah, *she* " spoke in her heart——But your little ones, which ye said should " be a prey, *them* will I bring in——Your carcasses, *they* shall fall " in this wilderness." I am well aware that this has been called an emphatical mode of expression; and, in some instances, accounted a particular beauty; as when the people exclaim, 1 Kings xviii. 39. " The Lord, *he* is the God; The Lord, *he* is the God." Be it so; yet, even here it has all the air of vulgar tautology; and brings to one's mind the old song: " Bell, *she* is my darling, &c." Were it at all deemed necessary to translate the redundant word for the sake of emphasis, I should prefer giving it another turn, and say, " That " woman, &c. The Prophetess Debora, &c.—Those little ones, &c. " —Jehovah himself, &c."—Although, in general, it would, per-

---

* We should laugh at a translator who should thus literally render: *Quid tibi vis? Scire ubi nunc sit tua tibi Daphnis?* or the French Je m'en vais—battez—moi cet homme-la va-t-en, il s'en est allé. Yet the personal pronouns are not less redundant in the above Hebrew phrases, than in any of these.

haps, be more agreeable to the fimplicity of the Scripture-ftile to leave the pronoun untranflated. *

>*Hoc quoque, Tirefia, præter narrata, petenti*
>*Refponde———*

A fimilar redundancy is frequent in the pronominal fuffixes ו and ה ; הם and הן ; efpecially in combination with the infeparable prepofitions ב and מ—" I know *him* that he will command his children " —the land which I will give you to inherit *it*—But of the tree of " the knowledge of good and evil, thou fhalt not eat of *it*. " Thefe are the nations, which the Lord left to prove Ifrael by *them*."† In many inftances our tranflators difregarded fuch expletives; thus Numb. xxxv. 34. inftead of " Defile not therefore the land which " ye fhall inhabit, which I dwell in *it*;" they judicioufly render " wherein I dwell:" and I can fee no good reafon why they did not extend the fame licence to all fimilar cafes.

It likewife appears to me, that it would often be proper to omit tranflating the relative אשר, efpecially when it cannot be rendered

* Our tranflators did not always render it. Thus Exod. iv. 14. we have, " I " know that he can fpeak well;" which in the original is, " I know that he can fpeak " well, *he*," correfponding exactly with the French vulgarifm, " Je vous le dis, moi— " il fe tait, lui."

† The French have a fimilar pleonafm. *La victoire* qu'il tient deja, un coup de fabre eft fur le point de *la* lui ravir. The victory, which he already grafps, the ftroke of a fabre is on the point of fnatching *it* from him. And fome of our modern refiners have fhewn a ftrange inclination to ape this ungrammatical mode of expreffion.

" without

without an italic fupplement. A ftriking example occurs in the very firft chapter of Genefis, v. 7. " God made the firmament, and " divided the waters which *were* under the firmament, from the " waters which *were* above the firmament." This is in reality a contradiction; for .if the waters were already above the firmament, what need to divide them from thofe that were below? Other tranflators have, with nearly equal impropriety, fupplied the word *are*; for how could the waters above, which God at the creation feparated by the atmofphere from thofe below, be the waters that are now feparated by that fame atmofphere? But if we tranflate fimply and indefinitely, " the waters above the firmament from the waters be- " low the firmament ;" all will be clear and confiftent.

The word איש, *man*, is often a mere expletive, not only in Hebrew, but alfo in Greek ; * and as fuch our tranflators fometimes confidered it. Exod. ii. 11. " He fpied (a man) an Egyptian " fmiting (a man) a Hebrew:" and v. 14. " Who made thee " (a man) a prince and a judge over us?" Judges vi. 8. " The " Lord fent (a man) a prophet:" xx. 4. And (the man) " the " Levite." † Why did they not ufe the fame freedom, Gen. xlii. 30. where they render איש אדני ארץ " The man who is the

---

* Μαχεδων ανηρ. Demoft. and in the New Teftament ανορες αδελφοι, αδελφης εταιροι, &c.

† In Jeremiah xxxviii. 7. they give it another term, and tranflate איש כרים one of the Eunuchs.

" Lord

"Lord of the land," at the expence of introducing two words that are not in the text*: and again v. 33. "The man, the Lord of "the country." I need not remark that אשה, *a woman,* is often in the same predicament. See 2 Sam. xv. 16. 1 Kings iii. 16. Jerem. iii. 3.

What I have said of איש is applicable to בן: "The sons of the "prophets," and "the prophets" are the same thing; as in Greek υιες Αχαιων and παιδες ιατρων signify only "the Greeks" and "the "Physicians:" and here a question might be made, whether it would not conduce to perspicuity, and prevent misapprehension, every where to render בני, except when it denotes the immediate progeny, by the gentile, or patronymic, of the proper name that follows? So that, instead of saying "the children of Reuben, the "children of Gad, the children of Moab, Amalek, Ammon, &c." we should say, "the Reubenites, Gadites, Moabites, Amalekites, "Ammonites, &c." Here, too, our translators have set the example; though, as I have already said, without any sort of uniformity. Joel iii. 6. "The children of Judah, and the children of "Jerusalem, have ye sold unto the Grecians." The Hebrew has "to the children of the Greeks." So Judges xix. 16. "Benjamites (it should be Benjaminites) for sons of Jemini." 1 Chron. xxiii. 27. "Levites" for "sons of Levi." 2 Chron. xxvii. 5. "Ammo- "nites" for "children of Ammon." Ezek. xxiii. 15. "Babylo-

---

* According to their scrupulous system, "who is" should have been in Italics.

"nians"

" nians" for " children of Babylon;" and even " men" for " sons " of man or Adam." Pſalm lxxxix. 47.*

This licence ſhould, I think, be extended to proper names, when theſe ſignify a whole tribe or people. This has been ſometimes done by our tranſlators, but not nearly ſo often as it ſhould ſeem expedient. A man of ordinary comprehenſion, on reading theſe words, " Judah " went with Simeon his brother—Judah took Gaza—The Lord was " with Judah; and he drove out the Canaanites—The Lord deliver- " ed them into the hand of Midian—Thus ſaith the Lord of Hoſts : " I remember what Amalek did to Iſrael; how he laid wait for him " in the way"—might naturally enough imagine that ſo many different individuals were here deſigned. Would it not be better, therefore, to tranſlate Amalekites, Midianites, Simeonites, Judaites?" or, if in the two laſt inſtances the terms may ſeem uncouth, ſupply in Italics the word tribe? Nor would I make the ſame exception here in favour of ישראל itſelf, that I juſt now made in favour of בני ישראל ; but I would render it " Iſraelites" when I ſaw occaſion ; or ſupply the word children.†

E 2   The

---

* I ſhould, however, I know not well for what reaſon, be inclined to make one exception : I would ſtill ſay, the children of Abraham, of Iſaac, of Jacob, and above all, " the children of Iſrael." It is a kind of national diſtinction of the poſterity of thoſe three patriarchs, and is ſo often repeated and ſo univerſally underſtood, that no ambiguity can eaſily ariſe from it.

† What has been ſaid in this and the preceding ſection is to be underſtood chiefly of the proſe parts of the Bible. In poetry, a different mode of rendering ſhould generally

The word פנים or פני is, likeways, sometimes pleonastic, though not so frequently, I suspect, as some Grammarians would have it to be. I see no reason for suppressing it in such phrases as these: "Darkness *was* "upon the face of the deep—There went up a mist from the earth "and watered the whole face of the ground—and behold the face of "the ground was dry." We daily use the word *face* in much bolder and far less analogical metaphors, and in reality, פנים signifies the external appearance of any thing. It is true, however, that the word cannot, in many places, be rendered literally; or should not, perhaps, be rendered at all: and in this the translator must be guided by grammatical analogy and idiomatical propriety; and follow, according to the particular exigency, that method of rendering, which is the most likely to give the full force of the original, without its obscurity.*

The

rally prevail; even although an explanatory note should be requisite to prevent mistakes.

* Beside the pleonasms which our translators introduced into the English Bible from the originals, they seem to have admitted others that have little or no foundation in the originals. For example, in rendering the second persons of the imperative mood, they have often expressed the personal pronoun *thou* and *ye* when they are not in the Hebrew. Thus, Num. xvi. 19. "Only rebel not ye against the Lord; neither fear ye the people of the land." It may indeed be said that *ye* is implied in the verbs: but surely it is not necessary to express it; and if אתם had been in the Text, they could have done no more. At any rate, if it was implied there, it was equally implied in the last part of the same verse; which is nevertheless rendered "fear them not." OF is plainly superfluous and, moreover, a solecism, in such phrases as these: "Take an heifer OF three years old. A lamb OF one year old," &c. Are not, likeways, all the personal

pro-

The same rules must direct him in rendering or not rendering יוֹם. קוֹל. דָּבָר. שֵׁם. קֶרֶב. תּוֹךְ. יָד. כִּי. פֶּה. &c. and how far, if he depart from the Hebraism, he may lawfully vary its equivalent. Let us now proceed to queries of a different nature.

It is well known that the singular number is, in Hebrew, very often used to express the whole genus or species of the thing signified. Such Collectives are more or less frequent in every language, but are of much greater extent in the Asiatic, than in the European dialects. " The earth brought forth—the herb yielding seed—and " the tree yielding fruit—And God made the beast of the earth after " his kind—Have dominion over the fish of the sea and over the fowl " of the air—Of every clean beast thou shalt take to thee by sevens." Our translators did not always think themselves obliged to follow so literal a mode of rendering. Gen. xxxii. 5. " I have oxen and asses." Hebrew, " I have ox and ass." Levit. xi. 2. " These are the beasts which ye shall eat." Hebrew, " This is the beast." Num. xxi. 7. pronouns too frequently repeated, when there is no real change in the person. I should, also, think that the word *that* is superfluous in such phrases as this, Jud. ii. 20. " And he said because *that* this people &c." יַעַן אֲשֶׁר and similar combinations being perfectly rendered by *because*. In like manner לְעַד and לְעוֹלָם seem fully rendered by " for ever," without the addition of " more." Nay a useless pleonasm may sometimes arise from the very arrangement of a sentence: and I think there are no less than five superfluous words in the following verse, Levit. xx. 2. " Whosoever HE BE of the " children of Israel, or of the strangers that sojourn in Israel, THAT giveth ANY of " his seed UNTO Moloch, he shall surely be put to death." Read it without the words in Capitals, and see if it be not as complete, more simple, and less embarrassed. Nor is there a single word of the Hebrew unexpressed : for the אֲשֶׁר before יִתֵּן is included in the word " whosoever :" neither is there any need of Italics to connect the sentence.

" Pray

" Pray unto the Lord that he take away the serpents from us." Hebrew, " the serpent." Surely they might have used the same freedom in many other places, which would have prevented a considerable number of ungrammatical combinations, which, by following the other mode, they could not easily avoid. I should therefore hope that no future translator will be blamed for rendering all such singulars in the plural number, unless when the word כל precedes them; in which case it will much depend on circumstances, whether he shall or shall not prefer the singular. I need hardly add, that the same liberty should be taken with plurals, when they convey only a singular meaning.

Beside this enallagé of numbers, which is extremely frequent, there is another of persons, the want of attention to which has introduced great confusion into modern translations, and given rise to many rash conjectural emendations of the text. It is, when in addresses to God, or even to man, the third person is elegantly used for the second ; and should always be rendered in the second. A proper instance occurs in Psalm civ. The Psalmist, in our common version, is made to address the Almighty in this manner : " O Lord
" my God, thou ART very great; thou ART clothed with honour
" and majesty. Who COVEREST thyself with light as with a gar-
" ment ; who STRETCHETH out the heavens like a curtain ; who
" LAYETH the beams of HIS chambers in the waters ; who MAKETH
" the clouds HIS chariot ; who WALKETH upon the wings of the
" wind;

" wind ; who MAKETH HIS angels spirits, and HIS ministers a
" flaming fire ; who *laid* the foundations of the earth *that* it should
" not be removed for ever: THOU COVEREDST it &c." Here,
besides that a look of incoherency is given to the whole passage, the
rules of our Grammar require STRETCHEST, LAYEST, MAKEST,
WALKEST, as well as ART, COVEREST, COVEREDST ; and the pronoun THY throughout, instead of HIS. But the affix ו after עליורי,
מלאכי, רכב, &c. determined our translators to admit a solecism rather
than depart from the letter of their original.

It is to be remarked that the Hebrew words, which are here
translated in the second and third persons, are, in reality, active
participles, and that, in such cases, it is a frequent idiotism of the
Oriental languages to express the agent in the third person, though
understood of the second. The Syrians go a step further and extend
this licence to the third person of the preterite. " O thou that
" SAID."—" O thou son of man who JUDGETH his neighbour."
—" Jerusalem, Jerusalem, that KILLETH the prophets and STONETH
" those who are sent to IT."* And so in the plural, " Tell me, ye, who
" are willing that THEY (not ye) be under the law." Nothing, then,
can be more just than St. Jerom's remark, that these and such enallages
create (to those who attend not sufficiently to the genius of

---

* The Greek has here partly the same enallagé—ἡ ἀποκτείνουσα τους προφητας και
λιθοβολουσα τους απεσταλμενους προς αυτην (not, προς σε) See also Luc. i. 42.—Act. xvii. 3.—
Rom. vii. 4.

the

the Hebrew language) innumerable difficulties; but if they be restored, as they should be, to their proper cases, persons and tenses, what appeared obscure will become plain and obvious*.

A difficulty here presents itself which has often puzzled me. In the injunctions which God gives to his people, the alternate change of numbers is extremely frequent, and often appears awkward in an English dress. " When *ye* reap the harvest of *your* land, " *thou* shalt not wholly reap the corners of *thy* field. *Ye* shall not " round the corners of *your* heads, neither shalt *thou* mar the corners " of *thy* beard.—If a stranger sojourn with *thee* in *thy* land, *ye* shall " not vex him—When a man or a woman shall commit any sin that " men commit, and *that* person be guilty, then *they* shall confess the " sin which *they* have done, and *he* shall recompense *his* trespass."†

---

* The enallagé that gave rise to this discussion is not peculiar to the Oriental dialects. It is quite familiar at this day to the Italians and Spaniards. Nor are we without examples of it in our own tongue.

" Oh thou, who TOUCH'D Isaiah's lips with fire."

In truth, our ideas are here divided between the personal pronoun and the relative. The latter is so generally connected with the third person, that we think any other connection unnatural. Thus when I say " Art thou the person who stole my watch?" I refer the relative to *person*, not to *thou*. So " thou who touched" is equivalent to " thou, the person, who touched."

† The same enallagé is often found where no precept is enjoined, particularly in poetical composition, although many such enallagés are, doubtless, chargeable on the Copyists, who frequently mistook and interchanged the suffixes. Examples may be seen in the blessing of Moses, Deuter. xxxiii. and in Psalm xvi.

Would

Would it, or should it be considered as dealing too freely with the Text, to reduce all that variety to one uniform tenor, and always translate such injunctions in the plural, except when they really are addressed to one person? The mode of translating which Broughton proposed, and which Castalio had, before him, adopted, would for the most part remove this difficulty; so much the more as our imperatives have no variety in termination; yet even this expedient would not always serve the purpose, as long as *thou* and *ye, thine* and *yours*, *he* and *they, his* and *theirs* are so often confounded. Besides, the future seems to give a solemnity and force to the precept, which is not so apparent in the simple imperative; and " Thou shalt not " steal——Thou shalt not commit adultery——Thou shalt not covet " thy neighbour's house, &c." would, I think, be ill exchanged for " Steal not"—" commit not adultery"—" covet not, &c." And, indeed, though in all other such cases, I should be inclined to use the plural; throughout the Decalogue I would retain the singular.

As idiomatical pleonasms may be retrenched in a translation without the smallest injury to the original author; so may his ellipses be with propriety supplied, if the supplements be virtually contained in the elliptical phrase. Putting such supplements in Italics, is a mere modern refinement, unknown to the most literal ancient translators. Even Pagninus himself did not dream of so silly a device. The father of it, I believe, was Arias Montanus; who yet, probably, never meant that it should be adopted in a translation for common

F

use.

use. His sole intention seems to have been to give to his half-learned readers some idea of the Hebrew idiom ; and that, indeed, is the only advantage that can be derived from his labour. It is therefore no small matter of surprise, that he should, in this respect, have become a model to posterior translators*; and continued to be so, until your Lordship broke the enchantment.

We should laugh at the man, who in rendering these words of Lucian, ȣ μοι σχολη, " I am not at leisure," should, to shew his strict attention and fidelity to the Original, distinguish the English words in this manner, " I *am* not *at* leisure :" which, after all, do not entirely exhibit the Greek idiom—Or who, of the Latin words " *Quid multa ?*" should thus variegate the version : " What *need is there for* many *words* ?" Or who, having to express in French the following sentence : " The news you bring are too good, not to " wish they were true ;" should deem it his duty, as a faithful interpreter, to put in Italics every word in his translation that has not a correspondent word in his original, even when the word is evidently understood, and might with equal propriety be expressed : " Les " nouvelles *que* vous apportez sont trop bonnes *pour* ne *pas* souhaiter " *qu'*elles fussent vraies."

* What is still more astonishing, some of those who translated from the Vulgate, paid the same scrupulous regard to its peculiar ellipsises ; although the author of the Vulgate was a free translator, and often abandoned the idiom of the Hebrew without necessity. But they thought, I suppose, that they could not, as Catholics, shew less respect for the Latin version, than Protestants had done for the Original.

But

But is it not as ridiculous in a Version of the Bible, to distinguish by Italics those necessary and implied supplements which we so frequently meet with in modern translations : " God saw that *it was* " good—This *is* now bone of my bone—These *are* the generations " of Noah—The men of Sodom *were* wicked. In those days there " was no King in Israel ; every one did *that which was* right in his " own eyes, &c." What else is this but to count syllables and play with words? Italics are not only often unnecessary, but, sometimes, degrade the Text. When Achish, for example (1 Sam. xxi. 15.), is made to say, " Shall this *fellow* come into my house." The word *fellow* is here worse than superfluous. It presents to the reader an idea that is not in the original ; and is, besides, a term not only low and vulgar; but also, if we attend to its etymology, improperly applied.

What has been said of the Pleonasm and Ellipsis, is more or less applicable to the Enallagé, Hypallagé, and other subordinate figures of speech, in the rendering of all which a translator should, I presume, be more studious of retaining the genuine sense than the precise idiom of his original ; when by endeavouring to express the latter, he would expose himself to the danger of obscurity, ambiguity, or barbarism.

I come now, my Lord, to a question of great importance, nearly connected with the preceding sections :———How far and in what circumstances is the Hebrew arrangement of words and sentences, to be followed in a translation ?

And here, I think, one general propofition may be laid down as incontrovertible; namely, That mode of arrangement is always the beft which expreffes the meaning of the original in the moft intelligible and energetic terms; and fuch as the author himfelf would, moft probably, have chofen, if he had written in the tranflator's language.

Luckily for an Englifh tranflator of the Bible, he will not be often under any great neceffity of departing much from the arrangement of the Hebrew; efpecially in the poetical parts of Scripture, where the two idioms are fo congenial as to appear almoft like twin-brothers*. Sometimes, however, he will fee ftrong reafons for changing the order even in poetry, and ftill more frequently in profe. This will happen either in the arrangement of the feveral words of a fingle fentence, or of the feveral members of a compound fentence, or of feveral different fentences together.

In the firft cafe it cannot be doubted, that it is not only allowable, but often neceffary to change the order of the Hebrew. There is hardly a verfe in the Bible, in which inftances do not occur. For, what Ainfworth, or other Englifh *Aquila*, would venture to fay, " In " the beginning created God the Heavens——And faw God the

* James's tranflators did not always avail themfelves of this natural advantage; and Purver almoft never attended to it.

" light

" light that it was good——The lamp of God before it went out——
" The labour of thy hands for thou ſhalt eat?*

It is little leſs indubitable, that the arrangement of the ſeveral members of a ſentence may ſometimes require to be changed. Thus Exod. xvii. 20. the order of the Hebrew is this: " He that ſacri-
" ficeth to other Gods, ſhall be utterly deſtroyed, ſave to the
" Lord only:" but our tranſlators judiciouſly changed that order, and rendered, " He that ſacrificeth unto any God†, ſave unto
" the Lord only, ſhall be utterly deſtroyed." So Exod. xii. 15. this ſentence, " Whoſoever eateth leavened bread from the firſt day
" until the ſeventh day," is in the Hebrew ſo arranged, that the laſt comma precedes the ſecond, which in Engliſh would be extremely uncouth and confuſed. In all ſimilar caſes therefore the arrangement of the original ſhould be departed from, and had our tranſlators more frequently done ſo, they would have left much fewer obſcurities in their tranſlation.

The only real difficulty, then, regards the third caſe. Is it lawful to tranſpoſe whole complete ſentences, when their natural order

---

* Yet even this mode of conſtruction our language admits: and it was often followed by our tranſlators. Then ſang Moſes—Then came Amalek—The right ſhoulder ſhall ye give, &c." *Quer.* would it not be better to reſtrain this inverted poſition of nominative and verb to interrogatory ſentences, and poetical compoſition?

† They followed the preſent faulty text; in which אחרים is wanting.

ſeems

seems to be inverted, and when there is reason to suspect that they have been shifted from their first place in the original?

That transpositions may have been made in the original texts of the Bible, as well as in other writings, will hardly be denied: nay, that they have actually been sometimes made is unquestionable: but I fear, some modern interpreters have been too ready to find them where they are not, or, at least, where there are not sufficient proofs or probability of their existing. I would therefore be extremely cautious in admitting them, and consider them nearly in the same light with a various lection. If there were found a diversity of order in the Hebrew manuscripts, or in the ancient versions, I should think myself at liberty to follow that order which should appear to me the most consistent with the context: but if all the manuscripts and versions agreed, I should be apt to look upon it as an original synchysis; and content myself with pointing out, in a note, a seemingly more natural order.

At the same time I confess, that I would not blame a translator for pursuing a different plan. For, provided there be nothing essential retrenched from the text, or added to it, I see no harm that can ensue from putting one sentence before or after another, on rational grounds*. Yet, as this licence, once assumed, would probably pro-

---

* *Quo ordine quid referatur, modo constat veritas, aut nihili aut parum interest.*
SCALIGER.

duce

duce too great a diverſity of arrangement (for almoſt every one would arrange in a different manner), I would rather be for retaining the preſent order in all ſuch caſes as admit only a doubt of its being the right one.

Before I diſmiſs this ſubject of arrangement, I will juſt remark, that tranſlators in general have paid too little attention to it. An improper diſpoſition of words in a ſentence, is little leſs offenſive to the eye and ear than confuſion in the ornaments of a building, or diſharmony in a piece of muſic; beſide its being productive of obſcurity, ambiguity, and even of a falſe meaning.—To the example I have given in my PROSPECTUS, from Ezek. permit me to add a few more from our laſt tranſlation. Judg. ii. 21. " I alſo will not " henceforth drive out any from before them, of the nations which " Joſhua left." Here the ſentence is embarraſſed by *any* being out of its place. Exod. xxxv. 29. " All manner of work which the Lord " had commanded to be made by the hand of Moſes." Here the meaning is ambiguous; and a ſmall change in the arrangement would have prevented that ambiguity. Gen. xiii. 10. " Lot lifted " up his eyes and beheld all the plain of Jordan, that it was well " watered every where, before the Lord deſtroyed Sodom and Go- " morra, as the garden of the Lord, like the land of Egypt, as " thou goeſt to Zoar." Here we are preſented with a wrong meaning; and the ſynchyſis of the Hebrew ſhould not have been fol- lowed

lowed in a vernacular verſion*. The ſame ambiguity is often found in the New Teſtament, from the ſame cauſe. For example, 1 Cor. xvi. 11. " With the brethren," is ſo placed that it may ſignify either that St. Paul looked for Timothy and the brethren; or that St. Paul and the brethren looked for Timothy:" By arranging thus, " For " I, with the brethren, look for him," the ambiguity is removed. Acts xxi. 5. " They all brought us on our way, with wives and children." Qu. whoſe wives and children? See alſo Acts xxii. 29. Romans iv. 16, 17, 18.

Beſide the general care with which a tranſlator ſhould arrange his words and ſentences throughout; ought he not moreover to aim at that diverſity of ſtructure which may be remarked in the different ſorts of compoſitions in all languages, and is ſtrongly diſtinguiſhable in the Hebrew writings? A poetical period will admit, and ſometimes require, an arrangement, that in proſe would be highly incongruous. Even in proſe there is, I conceive, a real, though not ſo ſtriking a difference, in the diſpoſition of the component parts of an hiſtorical ſentence, a precept, a parable, and an apophthegm. The laſt, in particular, ſeems to demand a certain degree of artificial neatneſs peculiar to itſelf; and which makes it the boundary, as it

---

* The laſt reviſers of the Geneva French verſion have well rendered this ſentence. " Lot ayant élevé les yieux, vid toute la plaine du Jourdain, qui étoit, avant que " l'Eternel eut détruit Sodome et Gomorra, arroſée partout juſq' à ce que tu viennes " en Tſoar, comme un jardin de l'Eternel, et comme le païs d'Egypte."

were, between prose and poetry; if it do not, indeed, belong to the latter.

At any rate, as Hebrew poetry is confessedly arranged in a very different manner from Hebrew prose, it is surely the duty of a translator to endeavour to imitate that difference in his version. And here it is, I think, that modern translations, our public one not excepted, are the most susceptible of further improvement. Your Lordship set the example; which has been successfully followed by Mr. Blayney and Bishop Newcome; and after which I also have attempted to form my imperfect copy.

But should a version of the poetical parts of scripture be divided into lines or hemistichs, corresponding with what is called Hebrew metre? This method, first practised by the Germans*, has been adopted by the writers of most other nations; and more especially by those of our own. Bishop Newcome has even made it one of his fifteen rules for a good translation.

Notwithstanding all this, I cannot help seriously doubting of its propriety. I can see no force or beauty it adds to the text, nor profit nor pleasure it can bring to the reader. On the contrary, I

---

* True it is, that we meet with a sort of stichical division, not only of the poetical, but likeways of the sentential books of scripture, in the Alexandrian and other Greek manuscripts; and we learn from Hesychius that this was an early invention: but I question if any of our modern metrical translators would take it for their model.

think, it confiderably disjoints and disfigures the one, and often perplexes and puzzles the other. Permit me to lay before your Lordfhip a fpecimen from your own Ifaiah; the firft that prefents itfelf.

> And it fhall be, when Moab fhall fee,
> That he hath wearied himfelf out on the high place,
> That he fhall enter into his fanctuary
> To intercede: but he fhall not prevail.
>
> Ifaiah xvi. 12.

Or the following from Bifhop Newcome's Zechariah:

> In that day Jehovah will defend
> The inhabitants of Jerufalem:
> And he that is feeble among them fhall be
> In that day, as David.

Does it really appear to your Lordfhip, that in either of thefe inftances the text looks to advantage; or that the reader will be better pleafed to fee it arrayed in this whimfical manner, than in the fober garb of meafured profe? I greatly fear he will not.

Indeed this mode of dividing a tranflation of the Hebrew poetry, feems very fimilar to that which was followed in the old literal Latin verfions of Homer; which not only give us no adequate idea of the beauties of the great original; but create an eternal difguft to the reader, by difplaying before his eyes all the external appearance of verse, without any of its properties. Yet those Latin lines have one advantage over your English ones: we are sure they correspond exactly with so many Greek verses; whereas no one will, I presume, assert the same of any stichical version made from the Hebrew.

You, my Lord, of all men know best, how little we are acquainted with the measure and mechanism of Hebrew verse; and how capricious, for the most part, are the divisions that have been made of them, even by the most learned Hebraists. What one would divide into long lines, another would divide into short; and what by this one would be combined into stanzas, would by that one be arranged in separate hemistichs. So that in reality, to give a version divided into lines of any sort, would be to give us no more than the arbitrary notions of the divider; and could only serve to impress a false, or at least an uncertain idea on the mind of the reader; without contributing either to his instruction or edification*.

For

---

* Such divisions are not only often arbitrary, but sometimes lead to delusion. I shall give an instance from Mr. Blayney's Jeremiah, Lam. ii. 17.

"Jehovah hath accomplished that which he had decreed,
    he hath fulfilled his word;
"What he constituted in the days of old, he hath destroyed and not spared."

To this construction he was "determined," he says, "by the metre." I should be glad to know by what rules of metre. Surely not by the parallelism, which is manifestly destroyed by this division——But let any one read the passage, without imagi-

For what instruction or edification can the mere English reader receive from such irregular and ill-connected lines as these, presented to him as an exemplification of Hebrew verse?

> In the house of Israel I have seen a horrible thing:
> There Ephraim committeth fornication;
> Israel is polluted.
> Moreover, O Judah, an harvest is appointed of thee
> Among those who lead away the captivity of my people.
> Zech. viii. 21.

Or these:

> And the inhabitants of one city shall go
> Into another, saying:
> Let us surely go to entreat the face of Jehovah,
> And to seek Jehovah God of Hosts:
> I will go also.

nary laws of metre in his head; and I am confident, he will naturally divide the words with all the ancient translators, in the following manner:

> Jehovah hath done—what he had devised;
> Hath accomplished the purpose—which he decreed of old;
> Hath destroyed—and hath not spared——

Not to mention that Mr. Blayney's last line presents an ambiguity, which a common reader might easily conceive to be a flat contradiction. " He hath destroyed and not " spared, what he had constituted in the days of old." What? had he destroyed his own decrees? It is certain that is not Mr. Blayney's meaning; but his meaning is not so obvious as it should be; and even if his construction were allowed to be right, perspicuity required that " What he constituted in the days of old," should be included in a parenthesis; or the word *what* changed into *as*.

Were

Were the text for public service to be thus divided, the best readers would, I believe, make but an awkward appearance in delivering the most sublime oracles of religion. The eye and the ear would be at continual variance; the tones and cadences would be perpetually confounded, and grating disharmony attend the pronunciation of almost every period.

On the whole, then, may I not appeal to your Lordship's judgment, even from your own practice; that in giving a version for general reading, such a division of those parts which are supposed to be poetry, would be attended with manifest inconvenience; and with no visible advantage; and that, therefore, a plain prose-like version, which should preserve as much as possible of what your Lordship has so ably proved to constitute the essence of Hebrew poetry, would be greatly preferable.

The Public will, perhaps, here, tax me with presumption for offering to differ from so many learned men. But I trust I have done it with all due deference and modesty. I have candidly proposed my own doubts; I wish to have them canvassed; am ready to hear what may be said on the other side of the question, and disposed to give up my opinion to the general voice.

Although a proper arrangement of words and sentences will, certainly, go a great way towards removing a number of ambiguities, it will not always be found sufficient to give to a translation of the Bible,

Bible, that degree of perspicuity, which a book intended for general instruction seems to require: and, therefore, every other mean should be employed, that can serve for that purpose, without hurting the integrity of the text, or altering its genuine meaning. Among these means I would propose the following licences, all which have already been taken by some one or other translator; and the greatest part of them by those even who profess to give the most literal versions.

Among the causes of ambiguity in the Hebrew text, one is, the too frequent use of the verb, without its proper nominative expressed. Thus Num. xxiii. 4. " And God met Balaam; and he " said to him, I have prepared seven altars, &c." The meaning, which the context only leads us to, would be more obvious, if the ו before יאמר were rendered " who," as was often done by the author of the Vulgate, and not unfrequently by some of the most scrupulous modern translators. Our own, sometimes, though rarely, used this licence. Thus Judges iii. 19. " But he himself (Ehud) turned " again from the quarries that were by Gilgal, and said, I have a " secret errand to thee, O King; WHO said (ויאמר) keep silence." And Jerem. xxxvi. 32. " Then Jeremiah took another roll and gave it to Baruch the Scribe, the son of Neriah, WHO wrote (ויכתב) therein, &c." See also Judg. iii. 31. Prov. xi. 22.—Why not extend it to all similar cases? It is indeed hardly conceivable how many obscurities and ambiguities are made to disappear by this single licence.

Another

Another mean has been employed to remove this species of ambiguity; especially when the verb repeated is אמר. When the second or third ויאמר has a different (though not expressed) nominative from the preceding one, St. Jerom very often, our first translators frequently, and our last not seldom render it " he answered ;" which not only excludes all doubtfulness of meaning, but breaks that colloquial monotony, which arises from the constant return of ". he said," and " he said" again*.

Yet neither of these expedients will always take away the ambiguity. Thus Num. xxiii. 7. " And he took up his parable." Who took up his parable? Not the person last mentioned in the text, for that was the King of Moab; but Balaam, mentioned in the preceding verse. Would it not be better then to insert *Balaam* in Italics before " took up his parable ;" so much the rather, as almost all translators, from the Seventy downwards, have, in other places not more ambiguous than this, taken the like freedom.

There is yet another method, which, if discriminately used, might serve to give a greater degree of clearness to the text, and at the same time prevent a tedious repetition of the copulative. It is to change the first of two or more consecutive preterites into the participle of the same verb. So, often, the Greek trans-

---

* Sometimes the Vulgate, for the sake of variety, joins this expedient with the former. *Et ecce Angelus Domini de cælo clamavit dicens: Abraham! Abraham! Qui respondit* (ויאמר) *adsum.* Gen. xxiii. 11.

lators.

lators. λαβουσα του καρπου αυla, εφαγεν—προσκαλεσαμενος δε Ισαακ τον Ιακωβ, ετει. εξαρας Ιακωβ της ποδας, επορευθη. And still more frequently the Vulgate: *Egreſſuſque Cain a facie Domini, habitavit, &c.—Bibenſque vinum, inebriatus eſt.—Incedentes retrorſum, operuerunt verenda patris ſui.—Reverſus invenit ſtantem Balac*, &c.

Although our laſt tranſlators ſeldom adopted this method, they very often took another equivalent to it. Of two copulatives they ſuppreſſed the one, and rendered the other by *when*; putting the ſubſequent verb in the preterpluperfect tenſe. Inſtances may be ſeen in almoſt every chapter. The Arabic and other ancient verſions had given them a precedent.

As the omiſſion of the nominative before its verb often begets ambiguity, ſo the too frequent repetition of it produces a diſagreeable tautology. In ſuch caſes the reſpective pronoun, it ſhould ſeem, might be uſed inſtead of it, when there is no danger of miſtake. For this too we have the ſanction of the ancient verſions, particularly the Vulgate; and even our firſt Engliſh tranſlators: but the maforetic ſuperſtition of poſterior times made our laſt reviſors afraid to follow their example.

The Hebrews have a peculiar mode of expreſſing themſelves in a negative manner, which is equivalent to a very ſtrong affirmation, but of an oppoſite nature. Thus, " not to heal one" is " to inflict " ſores on one."—And " not to find a thing" is " to loſe it."—In

all

all such phrases, I am of opinion that the meaning, not the words, should be attended to; and the phrase rendered equivalently. Take an example from Hosea xii. 8. " All his labour shall not be found " to him" (which is Bishop Newcome's translation of a corrected text) is, doubtless, equivalent to " All his labours shall be lost." Would it not therefore be better so to translate, than be under the necessity of making out the sense by the aid of a word in Italics; which, after all, presents an ambiguous meaning? " All his labours " shall not be found *profitable* to him." *Some* of them, then, may be found profitable.

There is yet another negative mode of expressing an affirmation, more common still than the former, introduced by the interrogative particle הלא or הלוא* " Are not they beyond the Jordan?" " Have not I commanded thee?" " Is not the arrow beyond thee?" " Are not these things written in the books of the Chronicles of " the Kings of Judah?" In such phrases, I presume, the affirmative may be used at the discretion of the translator; and will often be preferable to the negative.

The remaining part of my queries regards, either certain Hebrew words, which, though their meaning be sufficiently known, seem to have been improperly rendered in English; or English words, which, though they were, perhaps, originally, as proper terms as

---

* *Negativa addita interrogationi adfirmandi vim habet; idem est quod omnino.* Tympius, Note in Noldium.

the language afforded, are not quite so consonant with our present ideas, or agreeable to the rules of our present improved Grammar— Or, in fine, such expressions as may seem profane or indelicate, if literally understood.

At the head of the first class I shall place אלוף, which our translators render " a Duke." As this word is, among the people, understood to denote only a certain order of nobility; would not the meaning of the Hebrew be better conveyed by the generical term *Chief* or *Prince*?

The word נפש, which in its primary signification denotes the vital principle, whatever it be, that makes matter capable of vegetation, increase, sensation, &c. is, in the Bible, chiefly appropriated to animal life; and more particularly to that of the human species. Our translators commonly rendered it *soul*; and, in many places, that may be deemed no improper rendering, especially in poetry; but, in general, I think, it should be translated *person*; and with the pronominal suffixes, often left untranslated. This, I am persuaded, would prevent many misconceptions of the true meaning of the text, as well as a number of false consequences deducible from such misconceptions. We cannot easily change the popular ideas that usage hath affixed to the terms of our own language; but we may frequently accommodate the terms of another language to those ideas. A philosophical dialect never existed, and probably never will exist.

4

As

As נפש is the vital principle itself, which in animals, according to the Hebrew phyſiology, reſides in the blood; ſo רוח, the natural meaning of which is *air* or *wind*, is tralatitiouſly uſed for animal reſpiration, or that portion of air which is neceſſary to keep the vital principle in motion, and which the Scripture calls emphatically " the breath of life," and thence it denotes what we call the whole ſpiritual part of man, or the human ſoul. By a ſtill ſtronger figure it is made to ſignify that ſupernatural influence by which the Deity is ſuppoſed to operate on his creatures, not improperly called divine inſpiration, or divine impulſe. In this ſenſe it is often perſonified, and called a *Spirit* either good or bad. Thus 1 Sam. xvi. 13, 14. " The Spirit of the Lord came upon David from that " day forward, but the Spirit of the Lord departed from Saul, and " an evil Spirit from the Lord troubled him." This is, perhaps, the boldeſt metaphor in the Oriental languages; and has given occaſion to many abſurd and ridiculous notions both among Jews and Chriſtians. It is, I confeſs, a very hard matter for a tranſlator to find terms adequate to all the various literal and figurative meanings of the word: but it ſhould be his ſtudy to ſeek them, and to make the beſt diſcrimination poſſible: ſo as not to preſent his reader with an idea that is not contained in the original. If he cannot always accompliſh this in the text, a ſhort explanatory note ſhould be added for that purpoſe.

Our tranſlators have often made a proper diſtinction in the rendering of this word; but ſometimes alſo they ſeem to have been led by theological fyftem to tranflate it *Spirit*, when fome other term would have been more fuitable. Your Lordfhip has moft properly corrected Ifaiah xiv. 7. But are there not many other fimilar paffages that ftand equally in need of correction? One in particular prefents itfelf at the very threfhold of the fanctuary, that has been long a ftumbling-block to thofe that entered. Gen. i. 2. ורוח אלהים מרחפת על פני המים "The Spirit of God moved upon the face of the waters." Although this tranflation greatly diminifhes the force and beauty of the narrative, is incompatible with the arrangement of the original context, and was rightly underftood and rendered by thofe of the ancient interpreters, who were the moft likely to perceive the general meaning of the Hebraifm; yet as the Seventy had literally tranflated it, and as it feemed favourable to one of the capital tenets of the Chriftian Church, it was eagerly adopted by almoft all Chriftian Expofitors, and generally applied to the Holy Ghoft. To make the text tally better with this application, the true fenfe of the word מרחפת was alfo perverted. It was remarked, it feems, by fome Syrian*, that רחף in that dialect might fignify *to brood*. This acceptation, which was itfelf but a figurative meaning at moft, was ftill farther improved into another figurative meaning; and thus, what was at firft only "a great wind agitating the waters," became in time the third perfon of the Trinity, hatching chaotic matter into life, as a bird does

* We learn this from St. Bafil; and fome have fuppofed that Syrian to be St. Ephrem. Ephrem, however, teaches quite the contrary.

her-

her eggs. Milton accordingly places him in that attitude, and makes him *with mighty wings outspread, sit brooding on the vast abyss.* This may be Poetry, but it is neither Scripture nor Philosophy. Another instance I shall give from the Psalms. Ps. civ. 4. is thus rendered by our last translators: " Who maketh his angels spirits, " and his ministers a flaming fire." That a servile translator from the Vulgate should be guilty of so egregious a mistake, is not, perhaps, to be wondered at. He had before him an ambiguous text; and might think it incumbent on him to be as obscure and unintelligible as *his* original; but that one who translates immediately from the Hebrew, and is but moderately acquainted with its genius, should so miserably degrade this sublime passage, is surprising indeed. " Who maketh the winds his messengers; and his ministers, the flashy lightning." A bold and sublime idea, and worthy an Oriental bard*

Although משפט is, in many places, properly rendered *judgment*, there are other places where, on account of the various acceptations of the English term, that rendering seems inadmissible. For example, Job xxvii. 2. אל הסיר משפטי is translated " God hath taken " away my judgment;" a meaning very different from that of the original, which evidently signifies " God hath put off my cause; " hath declined bringing me to trial." Our translators might have,

---

* Bishop Hare has well rendered this verse in Latin, *faciens Angelos suos, ventos; Ministros suos, ignem flammantem:* but Green, who took Bishop Hare for his model, has ill-translated into English the first line. " Who maketh his angels winds."

in

in some sort, removed the ambiguity, by rendering מִשְׁפָּטִי " my
" right," as they did in the sixth verse of the last-quoted chapter;
where " I lie against my judgment" would not present a more
incongruous meaning, than, in the former passage, " God hath
" taken away my judgment."

It cannot be too often repeated, that perspicuity is the chief
quality of a good translation; to attain which, it will always be
lawful for a translator to paraphrase what cannot be literally rendered without obscurity. From this principle your Lordship has
clearly and elegantly translated Isaiah xl. 27. " And my cause
" passeth unregarded by my God," which in our vulgar version
is perplexed and ambiguous: " My judgment is passed over from
" my God."

I also doubt if the words אָמֵן and אֱמוּנָה be always properly rendered *faithful, true; faithfulness, truth*; and I should be apt to think
that *veracious* and *veracity* might sometimes be fitly employed to express their meaning.

Is there any word in our language, or could any word be analogically introduced into it, that would, in any degree, express
the relation between מִשְׁפָּחָה and שֵׁפַח—or between שֶׁבֶט a *tribe* and
שֵׁבֶט a sceptre? I fear not.

The God of the Israelites is particularly distinguished by the
name יהוה; of which neither the precise meaning nor the genuine

pronun-

pronunciation is well known. *Jehovah* is a barbarous term, that was never heard of before the sixteenth century*; neither Pagninus, nor Munster, nor even Montanus, used it in their versions: but Junius and Castalio having once given it a sanction, it came gradually into general usage among Latin translators and commentators; and has of late made its way into vernacular versions†. Bate, your Lordship, Green, Blayney, and Bishop Newcome, have all adopted it; and the last-mentioned writer thinks it should always be used.

I have, notwithstanding, some doubt about it; which I beg leave to propose. As the word LORD has been so long employed among Christians, to denote the Supreme Being, and is the only one in the New Testament by which he is known, I should be strongly inclined to retain it in the Old; so much the more, because the ancient Greek, Syriac, Latin and Arabic interpreters respectively rendered יהוה by a similar term Κυριος, מריא, Dominus, רב. Besides, we sometimes meet with יהוה in construction with צבאות: which we could hardly render " Jehovah of Hosts;" and Bishop Newcome himself allows that, in such cases, we must supply אלהים and say " Jehovah God of Hosts."

* Drusius could find no higher authority for it than that of Galatinus.

† I know not, however, if it have yet been admitted into any vernacular versions except that of Michaelis in German. Luther's, the Dutch, Danish, Old Swedish, Italian, and Spanish have *Lord*. The French Genevan has the *Eternal*, which has been adopted by the Paris Capuchins in their late translations.

There

There is only one objection that now occurs. The word אדון is alſo tranſlated *Lord*, and with the ſuffix *my Lord*, although it is only a term of reſpect applied to human beings; and moſt probably never applied to the Deity without the repetition of האדנים, " Lord " of Lords*." It ſhould ſeem, therefore, that a diſtinction ſhould be made between the terms. Our tranſlators made a diſtinction. They rendered יהוה THE LORD, and put it in capitals; and אדוני *my Lord*, in common letters. If a farther diſcrimination be deemed expedient, let ſome other term be uſed to expreſs אדוני; and I ſee no one ſo proper as *Sir*. It will, perhaps, be ſaid that the term is too trite and familiar; but it is not more ſo than אדוני muſt have been in Judea; nor can it, on that account, be more improper in the Old Teſtament than in the New; where we have " Sir, thou " haſt nothing to draw with," John iv. 11. And in the ſame chap- " ter, " Sir, give me this water.—Sir, I perceive thou art a pro- " phet.—Sir, didſt not thou ſow good ſeed in thy field, &c." And in the plural, Acts xxvii. 21. " Sirs," (ſaid St. Paul) " ye ſhould " have hearkened unto me;" and v. 25. " Wherefore, Sirs, be " of good cheer." The Greek indeed is here ανδρες; but if the

---

* In the preſent Maſoretic text, indeed, and even long before the exiſtence of the Maſora, we frequently find אדוני for יהוה (though with conſiderable variation in the manuſcripts); but we owe this, I ſuſpect, to the ſuperſtition of the Jews. There is not a ſingle inſtance of it, I believe, in the Samar. Pentateuch. See a curious paſſage relative to this matter in Mr. White's tranſlation of the *Preface to the Arabic Hexa- plar Pentateuch*, in the Bodleian Library—Letter to the Biſhop of London, p. 22.

Apoſtle

Apostle had spoke in Hebrew, it would have been אדוני. At any rate, the term has the authority of our last translators. Nay, we meet with it, once at least, in the Old Testament. "O Sir," (said Joseph's brethren to the Steward) "we came indeed down at the first time to buy bread." Gen. xliii. 20. I would therefore propose using, throughout, the word LORD for יהוה, and the word Sir* for אדוני.

It has been well remarked by Le Cene and others, that *naked* is often too strong an expression for ערה; and yet, perhaps, we have not in our language a suitable modifying term. The same observation is applicable to דרש. זנה. ידע. עלה. פקר. קום. ענה. בעל. ברך, &c. which we often find it impossible to render with that degree of propriety we wish: Is not Horace's maxim, then, of *innovating a little* here applicable? And might not a translator be allowed to borrow from other languages such terms as are easily convertible, and readily understood; or to revive such obsolete ones of our own as would express the meaning with more discriminating accuracy; or, in fine, to extend occasionally the acceptation of words now in

* This, however, can only be done when אדוני is in the compellative case — for we do not say, *My Sir* such-a-one, as the French and Dutch do; nor even *Sir* such-a-one, as the Italians and Spaniards do: and therefore we must, in all other cases, render it either *My Lord*, or *My Master*: for Mr. would hardly be sufferable in a translation of the Bible.

use, where there is no danger of error or confusion by such extension*.

Of English terms, that may have been proper enough at the time our translation was made; but which now seem to convey either a different meaning, or a meaning not quite so characteristical as others that have been since adopted, I shall content myself with giving the following, as examples.

Our translators were led to render וראיתן על האבנים, Exod. i. 16. "And see them upon the stools;" from its being then customary to deliver women on a sort of stool made for the purpose, and kept by the midwife. But, besides that it is extremely doubtful if אבן ever signify a stool; that practice being now generally discontinued in Britain†, and the expression "upon the stools," presenting an idea very different from that of *delivery*, should not the term itself be changed; or rather another turn given to the sentence, which

---

* Of this last kind of licence, I will just propose one example: "To *divide* light from darkness" has always appeared to me a term not sufficiently proper to express the true meaning of בדל in this phrase. The Latin *distinguo* seems much more suitable. Why then might we not use the word *distinguish* in the same signification? So much the rather, because that is really its primitive meaning, although it has gradually lost it, and is now seldom used but in a metaphorical sense. Your Lordship's approbation would go a great way to embolden me in taking a few such licences. See some sensible reflections on this subject in Maty's Review for June 1786.

† The practice is still used in Holland and other northern nations; and even in the Royal Lying-in Hospital of Copenhagen. See Medic. Comment. Vol. IV.

should

should sufficiently express its meaning without being liable to future misconception?

Audience formerly signified the *act of hearing*; and so it was used by Milton; but as it now seems obsolete in that meaning, should we not substitute *hearing* in its stead; and translate Gen. xxv. 10. " And Ephron the Hittite answered Abraham in the hearing of the " children of Heth?" *Travail*, too, for *labour* is become altogether obsolete. Yet both Bishop Newcome and Mr. Blayney have retained it. " Get you to the mountains—Get you hence—I will " get me unto the Great One;" and such-like expressions appear also to be justly going into disuse; and have moreover an imperious and vulgar air.

Peradventure is a word which we have no occasion for; and which is now hardly ever used.

I have, elsewhere, given it as my opinion, that words which we have once fairly adopted from other languages are, for the most part, more noble, more expressive and discriminating than our own original ones. Thus, I think, to *assemble* is better than to *gather together*; *convoke* than *call together*, *gratuitously* than *freely*.

Meat-offering was never the most proper term for מנחה, but is now still less so from the more limited acceptation of the word meat.

To *discover*, or *uncover*, seems sometimes used in a sense which it will hardly bear. Thus Nahum iii. 5. " I will discover thy skirts " upon thy face." Or, as Bishop Newcome renders, " I will uncover " thy skirts before thy face." We cannot, I think, say with propriety to *uncover* the thing *covering*, but the thing *covered*. Some other term, therefore, should be found to express the Hebrew word גלה, both here and in other similar places.

Exalted seems to be improper, when applied to material objects, as " Every valley shall be exalted." Isaiah xl. 4.

The word *unto* seems frequently misused in our present version. It has there four different acceptations. For first, it marks the dative case: " *Unto* Adam he said." Secondly, it denotes motion to a place: " And Moses went up *unto* the mountains." Thirdly, it precedes the farthest extreme of local situation: " From the river " of Egypt *unto* the great river." Fourthly, it is placed before the last period of time: " Since the days of Joshua *unto* that day."— Now I should think that it is proper only in the second and third examples; but not in the first and fourth; where *to* and *until* appear to be more grammatical.

Are the words *wherefore, therefore, wherein, therein, whereof, thereof, whereby, thereby, whereunto, thereunto, heretofore, theretofore,* and other such-like compounds to be retained? To be convinced that they are not strictly grammatical, we have only to analyze them, for who could bear, *for there, for where, in where, in there, of where,*

where, of there, &c? And yet I fear we cannot well do without them, particularly the two firſt.

The word *there* is alſo frequently uſed in another manner, the propriety of which might be queſtioned; and where indeed it ſeems to be a mere expletive. Thus when we ſay, " There was a man " in the land of Hus:" we ſay no more than " A man was in the " land of Hus." And when we ſay, " Let *there* be light—Let *there* " be a firmament, &c."—We might ſay " Let light be—Let a " firmament be"—or even " Be light—Be a firmament."—And in the imperative mood we frequently uſe this more regular mode of expreſſion, eſpecially in poetry; but in the indicative, it would ſeem uncouth, and perhaps at firſt ridiculous, becauſe our ears are not accuſtomed to it.

Some think that the expletives, *do, doth, did,* are often a beauty, in as much as they add a particular emphaſis to the expreſſion; and your Lordſhip has given countenance to this opinion in your Elements of Engliſh Grammar. Is it founded in nature? and would not Gen. iii. 13. be as forcibly rendered, " The ſerpent beguiled " me, and I ate;" as " The ſerpent beguiled me, and I did eat?" It ſeems ſtill more ſuperfluous in ſuch texts as the following, Gen. vi. 17. " I do bring a flood of waters upon the earth." Gen. xxvi. 30. " And he made them a feaſt, and they did eat and drink." Exod. x. 5. " And they (the locuſts) did eat every herb of the field." In general, then, would it not be better to reſtrict it entirely to negative sentences; or at most to extend it to a concession or strong affirmation? Thus, Joshua ii. 4. might be rendered " There did come men unto me." And Gen. xviii. 15. is very properly " Nay, " but thou didst laugh."

Is the expression " to take to wife" reconcileable with any rules of grammar or analogy? And, if not, how are we to translate לקח לאשה? Dr. Gosset suggests " to take for a wife," as he thinks *to marry* would hardly be endured; yet our translators have used it in 2 Chron. xiii. 2. where they render וישא לו נשים ארבע־עשרה " and married fourteen wives." See also Gen. xix. 14. Num. xii. 1. and 1 Chron. ii. 21.

If we at all retain the word *beseech*, should not the preterite *besought* be at least exploded; and *beseeched* used instead of it?

Our translators, for the most part, carefully distinguished the nominative plural *ye* from the accusative *you*; should not due regard be still paid to this distinction, in spite of the propensity of our present writers to neglect it? Would you not also retain the termination *eth* in the third person singular of the indicative mood?

I would, also, fain persuade myself, that we should not confound nor use indiscriminately, the terms *lo* and *behold*. The former I would employ, when there is nothing in the narrative immediately pointed at; the latter, when some object is indicated as present.

fent. Thus I would fay, "Behold the man—Behold the Lamb of "God:" but "Lo! I bring a deluge—Lo! it was Leah—Lo! it be- "came a ferpent." So that *Lo* may be always confidered as a mere interjection; *Behold* as the imperative of a verb. Is this diftinction more than ideal*?

The definite article *the* feems to be often inferted where it fhould not be inferted. Thus Gen. i. 6. "God faid; let there be a firmament; and let it divide THE waters from THE waters:" It fhould be "Waters from waters," as our older tranflators have it. Deut. xx. 5, 6. "Left he die in THE battle," fhould be "Left he die in "battle;" and fo they have it in the next verfe. On the other hand, they have omitted it where it fhould not be omitted. Thus Ecclef. xxii. 6. "But ftripes and correction of wifdom," fhould be "The ftripes and correction, &c." Nor is this omiffion always of fmall moment. A notable example occurs, Rom. ii. 12. where the omiffion of the article not only mars† the meaning, but gives an air of

* This interjection, fo extremely frequent in the Hebrew writings, is fometimes rendered by the ancients, efpecially by St. Jerom, by an equivalent term. Thus Gen xxix. 25. for ויהי בבקר והנה היא לאה, the VULGATE has "facto mane *vidit* Liam." And SYR. וכד הוא צפרא וחוא דליא הי; and when the morning came, and *he faw* that it was Lia, &c. This licence, I think, may be occafionally ufed, particularly when the interjection is repeated in the fentence; and thereby embarraffes it. Sometimes a tranfpofition will have the fame good effect; and fometimes it may be accounted a pleonafm, and omitted.

† According to Johnfon this word is obfolete. But why is it obfolete? It was ufed by Shakefpeare, Milton, Waller, and Dryden; is a Teutonic, nay a Hebrew radical word; and even in its found more expreffive of the meaning than any of its fubftitutes. Let us not always be biafled by ufage or authority.

impiety

impiety to the paffage: " For as many as have finned without law, " fhall alfo perifh without law." This omiffion is the more remarkable, as in the counterpart of the fame verfe the article is properly reftored: " And as many as have finned in THE law, fhall be " judged by THE law:" that is, the law of Mofes.

Your Lordfhip's authority has greatly contributed towards reftoring the conjunctive mood to its original place, after the hypothetical particles *if, though, unlefs, except,* &c. and, confidering how little variety of termination our verbs have, I would by no means difpoffefs it of its juft claim. But thofe particles are not always hypothetical; and, therefore, to join them always with the fubjunctive (as many writers, who wifh to be thought more than commonly correct, affect to do) feems to be an impropriety. I would, with your Lordfhip, make this diftinction. When the phrafe is evidently conditional, expreffing a doubt or depending on a contingency, the fubjunctive fhould ever be ufed: but when a conceffion, which is equivalent to an affirmation, is included in the fentence, I would uniformly ufe the indicative. If this obfervation be allowed to be juft, it is plain that its application will be of great latitude.

There is nothing, I believe, in our language more undetermined than the ufe of the infeparable prepofitions *in* and *un*. The former is evidently borrowed from the Latin; and, in many inftances, retains

tains with us its Latin intenfive fignification: whereas the latter is of Saxon origin, and is always a privative. Since then we are poffeffed of a privative prefix of our own ftock, and fince it is perfectly fufficient for the purpofe, it may be pertinently afked, why we fhould not exclufively employ it to denote privation; and confine the other to fuch words only, as being derived from the Roman tongue, ftill retain their intenfive meaning in ours*? It will be faid, perhaps, that although this rule be eftablifhed on principles of general analogy, it muft neceffarily be liable to many exceptions. When the prefix coalefces with a word of which the initial is an *l*, an *m*, a *p*, or an *r*, euphony has introduced the ufage of changing the *n* of the prepofition into one of thofe letters: now it would be extremely harfh and uncouth to read and write *ullegible*, *unmeafurable*, *urrefiftible*, &c. That fuch a pronunciation and orthography would, at firft, appear harfh to the unaccuftomed ear, and ftrange to the unaccuftomed eye, I readily grant; yet there is, in reality, no more harfhnefs nor oddity in *ullegible* than in *nullity*, in *unmeafurable* than in *mummery*, in *urremediable* than in *currency*. But there is no need for introducing this novel form; feeing we have already fuch a multitude of words in which the *n* retains its own fhape and found, in words beginning with the forementioned letters; without our perceiving any degree of cacophony or incongruity.

---

* Examples: *infrigidate*, *infufcate*, *ingeminate*, *immerge*, &c. But this difference is better illuftrated by contraft: *incarcerate* and *uncarcerate*; *inchain* and *unchain*; *infold* and *unfold*, &c.

For surely we may say and write *unlegible* as well as *unlearned*, *unlettered*, *unlibidinous*; *unmeasureable* as well as *unmerciful*; and *unremediable* as well as *unrebuked*. And was not Shakespeare's *unreconcileable* (Anth. and Cleop. Act v. Sc. 1.) more proper and as harmonious as our *irreconcileable?* I wish our professed grammarians would take this matter into consideration, and give us some consistent principles to be guided by.

I have observed a mode of phrasing, that now seems to prevail; which, nevertheless, I am apt to consider as a real solecism. It is to suppress the little word *it* in such sentences as the following: " Now that this of the two is the better gloss, *it* is proved by your " own interrogation." So Chillingworth, and the writers of his time; but our moderns would, in imitation of the Latins, make the first part of the sentence the nominative to the verb; and write, " That this of the two is the better gloss, is proved, &c." Change only the order thus: " Now *it* is proved that, &c." and the necessity of retaining the *it* will be manifest.

Another still greater impropriety seems to be creeping in upon us, from our French neighbours; and is already found in writers of repute. It consists in beginning a sentence with an insulated nominative, which has no corresponding verb; as, " Born a poet, verses
" cost

" coft him nothing.—Irafcible beyond credibility, the fmalleft con-
" tradiction put him in a paffion." I know not if there be any
thing more oppofite to the genius of our language than fuch a con-
ftruction*.

Notwithftanding all that has been written by our moft recent
grammarians about *fhall* and *will*, *would* and *fhould*, it does not appear to me that there are yet any *criteria* eftablifhed to direct us in
the ufe of them. Your Lordfhip has juftly obferved that our an-
ceftors, even as late as the reigns of James and the Charlefes, re-
fpectively employed them in a different manner from that of the
prefent time; and I cannot help thinking that the ufage of our an-
ceftors was, in fome regard, preferable to ours.

In disjunctive fentences, fhould we ufe *or* or *nor* after *not* and *neither*? The nature of negatives feems to require *nor*; yet I have frequently obferved, even in thofe writers who affume to themfelves
the peculiar province of correctors general of ftile and grammar,
fuch expreffions as thefe: " *Neither* he *or* any one elfe.—*Neither* the
" one *or* the other of thefe affertions, &c." To me this appears ungrammatical.

* This cannot be called the *cafe abfolute*; becaufe the *fubject* is the fame in both
parts of the fentence; and the *predicate* and the *fubject* muft neceffarily be in the
fame cafe.

One query still remains about the orthography of proper names. Our first translators of the Bible, Tindal and Coverdale, retained the old pronunciation of the proper names, such as they found it in the Greek and Latin versions, with little variation and few exceptions. Thus they wrote *Heva, Noe, Jared, Mathusala, Nemrod, Ninevé, Cades, Cades-Barné, Bersabé, Booz, Isai, Elizeus, Salomon, Aggeus, Oseas.* In some instances, they followed the French form; *Esaye, Jeremie, Zachary, Abdy, Sophony,* &c. Sometimes they adopted the Masoretic mode of pronunciation; as *Zoar, Serug, Terah, Peleg,* &c. A farther approximation to this last form was made in Cranmer's and Parker's Bibles; particularly in those names that were less known, and consequently less apt to strike or surprise the people by a new sound, while the more celebrated were retained in their old orthography. But the English refugees at Geneva, taking the French Calvinists for their model, scrupulously adhered to the Masoretic punctuation, in their expression of the proper names, and as much as possible to the literal sounds of the Hebrew alphabet, such as modern grammarians exhibit them. James's translators generally adopted their plan, but with many modifications, either to avoid cacophony, or not to deviate too widely from the sounds to which the people had been so long accustomed. They did not, therefore, write *Methusael, Sheth, Enosh, Shem, Izhak, Jaakob, Rebekah, Rahel, Nashshon,* &c. Yet, in general, they followed the Geneva plan, both in this and most other particulars; as may be seen by any one who shall take the trouble to compare them.

Since

Since that period little innovation has been attempted in the Hebrew names, except by Bate, with whom *Henoch* is *Henuc*, *Jared Oirad*, *Adah Odeh*, *Zillah Jilleh*, *Enos Anujh*, *Chenaan Canon*, *Lot Luth*, *Zoar* or *Segor Juar*, *Ephron Oprun*, *Judah Jeudeh*, *Aaron Aorun*, *Zadok Jaduk*, *Bethel Bith-al*, &c. &c. Uncouth as this orthography may feem to be, it was, not without fome fpecious reafons, adopted by Bate. He wifhed to exprefs, as nearly as poffible, what he took to be the genuine original powers of each Hebrew letter, defpifing not only the Maforetic pronunciation, but alfo that of the moft ancient interpreters, who lived at a time when the Hebrew was yet a fpoken language. Now he fhould have, in this refpect, defpifed neither the one nor the other; but either have retained the proper names as he found them in the common verfion, or at leaft corrected them on better authority than his own capricious ideas.

Is it unexpedient then to make any change at all in the prefent orthography of the Hebrew proper names? I fay not that; but I think the change fhould be natural, analogical, and founded on orthography, reafon, or ancient authority. It were certainly to be wifhed that every name could be fo written in a verfion, as to be diftinguifhed even by its found, and exprefs, as nearly as poffible, the powers of the Hebrew elements that compofe it; and this has been more or lefs attempted by the moft wary and
cautious

cautious tranflators. But then the names muft not, even for this analogical difcrimination, be fo ftrangely metamorphofed, as not to be known again for the fame. This indeed will rarely happen, if we do not give a new pronunciaton to the vowel founds; I mean the real vowels א. ה. ו. י. ע. and their feveral combinations. Of all thefe, as it is impoffible to know precifely their various powers in the mouth of an ancient Jew, the beft we can do is to found them as they have been handed down to us, whether by the ancient interpreters or Jewifh grammarians; no great matter which. Thus though איוב would feem, if I pronounce each letter feparate, to be expreffed by Aiub (and fo Bate would probaby have written it) yet I will continue to call it Job, or at leaft Iob; becaufe I find all the ancients fo exprefs it; and because in reality there is nothing uncommon in thofe letters taking that found. In fact, if we pronounce *I* in Job as we do in *Iambicks*, we fhall give it the very found which the Italians give to *ai*; and if we pronounce the *o* as our *o* fhort, it will not differ from *u* fhort. Were our proper name *George* to be treated by an Oriental as we treat the Oriental names, and expreffed in thefe letters גהערנה, it would be fo altered as not to retain a fingle found of the original, excepting that of *r*.

I am therefore of opinion, that we fhould retain the old names with as little variation as poffible. The only innovations I would propofe are the following: The ח I would always exprefs by *h*; the כ by *ch*; the ק by *c* or *k*; the ש by *fh*; the ת by *z*; and the צ by *ts*,
or

or ς with a point above it. This would be sufficient to distinguish the similar consonant sounds. And as the *h* at the end of proper names ending with ה is useless, I would only retain it to distinguish masculines from feminines, as *Judah* from *Debora*, &c.

Before I leave the subject of proper names, I must observe, that we are now so accustomed to place the definite article before those of rivers and mountains, that they look, somehow, naked without it. Yet this mode has not yet, I believe, been introduced into any English version; and it would, perhaps, be by some accounted a blameable innovation to write " The Euphrates, The Nile, The " Jordan, The Chobar, The Lebanon, The Carmel, The Thabor, &c." Perhaps we should make a distinction. When the name mentioned is not attended with its appellative *river*, and is the nominative or objective of a verb, the article should be prefixed; but when *river* is immediately joined to it, or when it is in concord or regimen with another noun, the article should not be prefixed.

The orthography of a proper name being once fixt upon, it should be retained throughout the whole Bible, both in the Old and New Testament; although there may be a variety of lettering it in the originals. See Bishop Newcome's Preface to the Minor Prophets, p. xxxvi.

With

With regard to such expressions in the original Scriptures as, if translated literally, would offer to the mind of the delicate and pious reader offensive images; I make no doubt but your Lordship will agree with me, that they ought to be accommodated to our times and manners, and rendered with more freedom than any other passages. Exemplification here is unnecessary. But I should be glad to know, whether in this class your Lordship would include such phrases as the following, פתח את רחמה, בא אליה, ידע אשתו, כל פטר רחם, &c.

These, my Lord, are a part of the principal doubts and difficulties that have occasionally presented themselves during the course of my present labours. I lay them before your Lordship with all that confidence which your former encouraging countenance so naturally inspires. If health and leisure shall allow you but to glance them over, I am persuaded that a great portion of the mist will be dissipated by so clear and keen a ray. I wish not to give your Lordship the trouble of writing long remarks. The shortest hint of approbation or the contrary; a single *yes* or *no* on the opposite page, relative to any query I have put, or opinion I have ventured to give, will be a sufficient indication of your sentiment, and go a great way to make me cherish or abandon my own. Before next Michaelmas I hope to have

the

the honour of submitting to your perusal a whole volume of my translation. How happy shall I esteem myself, if it should have the good fortune to merit the same flattering approbation you were so kind as to express of my Prospectus. Whether that be in my fate, or not, I eagerly seize this opportunity of testifying to the Public, with what respect and veneration I have the honour to be,

MY LORD,

Your Lordship's

Much obliged,

And most obedient,

Humble Servant,

A. GEDDES.

LONDON,
January 15, 1787.

POSTSCRIPT.

EVER ready to own and rectify my mistakes, to supply omissions, or to answer rational queries, I take this occasion to make the following additions to my PROSPECTUS which was lately published; and in which I am sorry to find more typographical and other errors, than, on too slight a reading over of the sheets as they came from the press, I had occasionally observed.

Page 2, line 5, after *agreed upon*, add what follows:

A late ingenious Essayist* has, indeed, given it as his opinion, that a new translation of the Bible is not only unneccessary, but even dangerous, nay *extremely* dangerous; and that, instead of serving the cause of religion, it would tend to hurt it: and a more recent writer, of no common abilities, in the Monthly Review, has adopted and enforced the same sentiment. It may not therefore be improper to hear, and fairly appretiate, their arguments.

* Knox's Essays, Vol. I. No. 49.

In the firſt place, the "venerable antiquity" of our preſent public verſion is urged as a reaſon ſufficient for retaining it, with all its faults.—This, in the mouth of a Proteſtant, ſeems to be an odd ſort of argument. If a Romaniſt had uſed it in favour of his *Vulgate*, he would be inſtantly told, "That no age nor preſcription can authorize error; and that it is obſtinacy "to defend in any verſion, however ancient or venerable, what cannot be "rationally defended." In fact, the lapſe of thirteen centuries has given no more real value to the *Vulgate*, than it had when it firſt appeared; nor is our preſent public verſion more eſtimable now than it was an hundred and ſeventy-ſix years ago. If time could enhance the value of a tranſlation, Tyndal's would be preferable to James's; for it can boaſt at leaſt two hundred and fifty years, and a part of it two hundred and ſixty. And old Wicliff might ſhake his hoary locks, and ſay, "I have a much "better claim than either."

But it is further urged, "That independently of age, and the air of "veneration which it has thence acquired, our preſent verſion ought to "be retained for its intrinſic beauty and excellence. The language, "though it is ſimple and natural, is rich and expreſſive. The poetical "paſſages of Scripture are peculiarly pleaſing. The tranſlation of the "Pſalms abounds with paſſages exquiſitely beautiful. Even where the "ſenſe is not very clear, nor the connection of ideas at firſt ſight obvious, "the mind is ſoothed, and the ear raviſhed, with the powerful yet unaffected "charms of the ſtyle, &c."

Although this panegyric be ſomewhat *outré*, I am willing to ſubſcribe to it. But all thoſe beauties, in an equal degree, and ſome of them even in a greater degree, are found in our firſt verſions, and muſt be more or leſs found in every verſion of the Hebrew ſcriptures that is not a mere paraphraſe. The great merit of James's tranſlators did not certainly conſiſt in beautifying or meliorating the ſtyle of the former verſions, but in correcting their errors, and making a verſion more ſtrictly conformable to the letter, not always the ſpirit, of their ſuppoſed indefectible originals. Their

fidelity

fidelity and accuracy deserve great commendation; and that is almost all they have a just claim to. The style they found in their prototype; and the diction and phraseology they borrowed from their predecessors in translation: and it was well that they had such models; for their own preface evinces that their taste was none of the best. We have indeed some difficulty to believe that it could be written by the same persons.

What is *beautiful*, what is *excellent*, what is *melodious* and *ravishing* in the present version, should be undoubtedly retained by all future translators; but is there any reason for retaining its corruptions, its mis-translations, its obscurities, and its other acknowledged imperfections? I scarcely think that its most partial admirer will contend for this. The judgment made by Mr. Knox, from a comparison of a late version of Isaiah with that of the public translation, is not altogether just. He should have considered, that the intention of the learned Prelate, in giving that version, was to exhibit a specimen of Hebrew metre, clothed in a corresponding English dress, and representing as nearly as possible the measure, the construction, the air, and complexion of the original. From this, and from the novel and awkward appearance of so many unequal and unmeasured English lines, and the many unnatural breaks and unexpected pauses that thence ensue, it frequently happens, I confess, that the old translation is more pleasant to read; the order and arrangement, too, appear often to be more harmonious; and sometimes, though rarely, the terms seem more properly chosen. But how fully is all this compensated by the clearness, precision, and energy of the Bishop's version, and the many corrections of a faulty or mis-translated text? Let this version be taken out of its present form, and divided and arranged like plain poetical prose; and the least intelligent reader will, I think, be struck with the difference.

But the most specious objection is derived from the danger of scandalizing the Christian people, and weakening their faith, by presenting them
with

with a new or improved verſion of the Scriptures. "We have received the
"Bible" (ſays the ſame amiable writer) "in the very words in which it now
"ſtands, from our fathers; we have learned many paſſages of it by heart
"in our infancy; we find it quoted in ſermons from the earlieſt to the
"lateſt times, ſo that its phraſe is become familiar to our ear, and we
"ceaſe to be ſtartled at apparent difficulties. Let all this be called pre-
"judice, but it is a prejudice which univerſally prevails in the middle
"and lower ranks; and we ſhould hardly recognize the Bible, were it to
"be read in our churches in any other words than thoſe which our fathers
"have heard before us." — Again, "If the leſſons of the Church were
"to be read in different words from thoſe which they have heard from
"their infancy, their faith might be more endangered than by all the argu-
"ments of the Deiſts."

This is an old objection*; it was made by St. Auguſtine to St. Jerom. The people of that day, who had received from their fathers the Bible in the words of the old Italic tranſlation, were aſtoniſhed, and ſome of them ſcandalized, on hearing the new verſion read in the churches; and a certain African Biſhop raiſed a tumult in his congregation, by ſubſtituting *hedera* for *cucurbita* in the fourth chapter of Jonah.

Whether any of our good people would be as zealous for the word *gourd*, experience only can decide: but if ſuch ill-founded prejudices really exiſt among them, it is the fault of their teachers; and their teachers ſhould ſeriouſly labour to remove them. The people ſhould be taught (for they are not indocil) that it is to the meaning, and not the words, of Scripture—to the ſenſe, not the ſound, that they ought to attend—That a

---

* It is worth remarking, that objections of the ſame nature have been made againſt tranſlating the Scriptures at all. "A number of pious but weak Chriſtians will be ſcandalized,
"will have their faith ſhaken, will be perverted to hereſy; therefore let the Scriptures re-
"main locked up from them, to prevent theſe evils."

tranflation of the Bible, like all other tranflations, is fufceptible of further and further improvement—That the languages in which the Scriptures were originally written, are now better underftood than when the laft tranflation was made—That the originals themfelves have, by the diligence and labours of the learned, been reftored more nearly to their firft integrity—and that, by thefe means, a number of difficult paffages may be illuftrated, obfcurities removed, objections obviated; and the Divine oracles made more intelligible to every capacity. All this the people have a right to know; and, knowing all this, they will not only be not averfe to a new tranflation, but expect it with eagernefs, and receive it with pleafure; with a pleafure proportioned to their zeal and devotion. For as to that clafs of devotees, if fuch there be, who believe that our prefent verfion was written with the finger of the Almighty; and that to alter a tittle of it, is to be guilty of blafphemy, it would be worfe than weak to encourage their prejudices; it would be to abet a real blafphemy, for fear of incurring, in their extravagant ideas, the imputation of an imaginary one.

The truth is, as far as I have been able to learn, that the people in general are fufficiently fenfible of the expediency of a new verfion, or a thorough revifal of the old one. There are few, even of the loweft clafs, who have not heard of the imperfections of the public verfion; our preachers are conftantly correcting particular paffages in it. Bible-hiftories and Family-expofitors, without number, are difperfed all over the kingdom, in which many mif-tranflations are corrected, or pretended to be fo; and yet the people read them with avidity, and even with enthufiafm. In fhort, the prejudices of the people againft an improved verfion either do not exift at all, or are fuch as may be eafily removed, or deferve not to be regarded*. Indeed if the above objections had come from writers lefs refpectable, I fhould have paid no attention to them.

Taking

---

* That the prejudices of the people are not fo ftrong as Mr. Knox feems to think, and that they are not fo eafily fcandalized on hearing the Scriptures read in words different from the

Taking it for granted, then, that a new, or at least an improved version of the Scriptures is wanting, and wanted; it is my intention, in this Prospectus, to explore, &c.

Page 5. l. last, *inculcate to*; I am not sure but it should be *inculcate on*.

Page 8. l. 15. The word *unclinch* has been objected to as inelegant, I fear it is also improper; perhaps *undo* might be substituted.—In the note of the same page, for *aversion*, read *an aversion*.

Page 10. l. 16. for *last*, read *latter*.

Page 13. l. 26. for *exculpating them of*, read *exculpating them from*.

Page 16. l. 20. for *is*, read *be*.

Page 18. l. 20. for *that they could*, read *if they could*.

Page 20. reform the note thus — Three volumes of this work are now (1786) published. The first, beside a sensible preface, Canons, and *Clavis* or catalogue of the MSS. used by the author, contains various readings on Genesis, Exodus, and Leviticus—the second carries them to the end of Kings — the third contains the Prophets and Megilloth — and the fourth, which is now in the press, will contain the rest. It were to be wished that De Rossi had been less sparing of his various lections; for he has only given those which he deemed of importance: whereas we want to know the real state of his MSS. and thence to judge for ourselves what readings are important, what not.

---

the present translation, we have a daily and flagrant proof before our eyes; and that too with respect to a part of Scripture that is more frequently read and repeated than any other. The words, and even the style of the Psalms, in the book of Common Prayer, are more different from those in the Bible, than they can well be in any improved translation; nay, the very Decalogue itself is expressed in different terms; and yet I never heard that any one was scandalized at this difference, or in either did not recognize the Bible. The Bible must be sadly travestied indeed, in a translation, before it cease to be recognizable.

Page 29. for *Hexapla*, read *Polypla*.

Page 32. l. 22. read *septuaginta*.

Page 34. laſt line, for *minor poets*, read *minor prophets*.

Page 35. I have too raſhly adopted the general prejudice, that the editors of the Complutenſian Polyglott did not, in their edition of the Septuagint, adhere to their MSS. I am at preſent of a different opinion; which, I truſt, I ſhall be able to eſtabliſh on the ſtrongeſt intrinſic evidence.

Page 37. l. 13. after *ſmall octavo*, add, and laſtly at Leipſick, by Reineccius, in 1757, on a ſmall but elegant type, in 8vo.; with ſelect various readings from the Alexandrian copy.

Page 40. l. 10. after *completed*, add, It is hoped the learned editor will be requeſted and encouraged to give the reſt of this ancient MS. in the ſame form.—*Ibid.* in the next note, Borgia is called by miſtake *prefect of the propaganda*; it ſhould be *ſecretary*.

Page 44. l. 21. for *Dominican friars*, read *Auguſtinian friars*.

Page 48. l. 10. for *paraphraſe*, read *the looſeſt paraphraſe*; and add, in a note—As an example of this, take Gen. xlvii. 26. *Ex eo tempore uſque in preſentem diem, in univerſa terra Egypti, regibus quinta pars ſolvitur; et factum eſt quaſi in legem; abſque terra ſacerdotali, quæ libera ab hac conditione fuit.* Compare this with the original.

Page 57. l. 19. add, Indeed ſuch emendations are, ſtrictly ſpeaking, more than conjecture. They ariſe from a ſort of intrinſic evidence, of the negative kind at leaſt, which often is ſufficient to exclude all ſort of doubt, and almoſt always to force a rational aſſent.

Page 61. I had ventured to use the word *vocable*. Some have approved of it, as a term we wanted; others have objected to it, as an innovation.

Page 75. l. 1. for *was*, read *is*; and page 79. line last, read—was republished at Leipsick, with the Hebrew text, in two volumes in quarto, in 1740.

Page 82. l. 15. for *we are*, read *I am*.

Page 94. l. 4. after *text*, add, A striking example occurs, Exod. xxxii. 18, where there are no less than eleven words in Italics, which not only give no force to the passage, but present a false idea; for who would not think, on reading it, that the words *shout, cry, sing*, corresponded to so many plural participles, and were equivalent to *shouters, criers, singers?* See the place, and compare it with the original.

Page 98. l. 5. I have used the word *forces* in a meaning hardly admissible in English; read therefore *strength* or *abilities*.

Page 99. l. 2. Add, Mr. Dawson has since published the sixth and eleven following chapters of Genesis, on the same plan.

Page 100. l. 9. after *merit*, add, Particularly an anonymous one, printed for Millar in 1751; and that of Dr. Hodgson, just now published. *Ibid.* in the note, add, and the last number (No. IV.) contains more good remarks on particular passages, from Genesis to the Proverbs inclusively, than any work of the same size in our language.

Page 102. l. 3. " The synod of Thoulouse is called a diocesan synod:" this is an oversight; it was certainly a provincial synod: and the following is the odious constitution alluded to: *Prohibemus etiam, ne libros Veteris Testamenti aut Novi Laici permittantur habere: nisi forte Psalterium vel Breviarium pro divinis officiis, aut Horas B. Mariæ aliquis ex devotione habere*

habere velit; sed ne præmissos libros habeant in vulgari translatos, arctissimè inbibemus. Concil. Tholosan. cap. xiv.—It is worth remarking, that this same Council seem to have been the first authors of a religious Inquisition. See *Capitula*, 1, 2, 3, 4, 5, 6, &c. apud Labbe, tom. xi. p. 427.

Page 109. l. last, add, Wicliff's translation of the New Testament was published by Lewis, in folio, in 1731. His press-copy was collated with ten MSS. the principal various readings of which are marked in the margin. Beside the manuscripts of Wicliff's version, at Cambridge, Oxford, and in the British Museum, there is a beautiful copy of the New Testament in the Advocates Library at Edinburgh; and one of the seven Catholic Epistles in the University Library of Glasgow.

Page 113. l. 13. Reform the whole passage thus: The Abbé du Contant de la Molette has, since the year 1777, published the following works on the Holy Scripture: *La Genése Expliqué*, 3 vol. 12mo. *L'Exede Expliqué*, 3 vol. *Le Levitique Expliqué*, 2 vol. *Les Pseaumes Expliqués*, 3 vol. In all which works, though he has retained Calmet's version made from the Vulgate, he is continually correcting it either by the Hebrew text, or by the other ancient versions; and so far his work may be accounted a translation from the originals. The Journal des Sçavans of last year announces two new French versions of the Psalms; one in eight vol. 12mo. by Berthier, the other in two vol. by Bauduer, both said to be estimable works; and of which the latter is immediately made from the Hebrew.

Page 125. l. 24. in the note, efface *Durell*; he should not have been placed in such company.

Page 128. l. 28. read *energetic*.

These are the most important corrections and alterations that now it occurs to make. There are many other little inaccuracies of less note; particularly in the orthography of proper names, which the printer has strangely metamorphosed, morphofed, but which the learned reader is requefted to correct thus: *Amama, Doederlein, Oufeel, Maldenhauer, Villoifon, Meninfki, Semler, Bjornfthal,* &c.

I have now only to return my hearty thanks to thofe gentlemen, who, fince the publication of my Profpectus, have favoured me with their friendly advice and affiftance in the profecution of my arduous undertaking; and to anfwer fuch queries as have been made to me by anonymous correfpondents, to whom I knew not how, otherwife, to direct an anfwer.

To Sir William Jones, of Ramfbury, Bart. I am indebted for the early communication of a manufcript commentary on the whole Bible; in which, although there be not much criticifm, there is a great deal of good fenfe, and many pertinent reflections.

Mr. Bradley, of Oxford, befide feveral excellent remarks on particular paffages of Scripture, has favoured me with a complete verfion of Jeremiah; of which he will fee, in due time, that I have profited.

Mr. Winftanley, and Mr. Croft, of the fame place, will permit me to acknowledge my refpective obligations to them.

Mr. Dimock, of Gloucefter, has fent me his very judicious obfervations on a great part of the Bible; accompanied with fuch expreffions of friendfhip as I can never forget.

To the politenefs of Colonel Vallancey I owe fome curious obfervations, and the difcovery of a valuable fragment of the Greek verfion of Ifaiah, kept in the library of the Univerfity of Dublin.

From fome other gentlemen, who have not chofen to let themfelves be known, I have received fome ufeful hints which fhall be duly attended to.

The

The plan of a Commentary, suggested by *Erasmus*, from Dublin, would be an excellent one for a professed commentator; as far as a mere translator is concerned, he will find that I have followed it.

T. B. and a *Protestant Divine* (whom I have since found to be a respectable clergyman of the church of Scotland) seem surprised at the liberality of sentiment that pervades my *Prospectus*; but still have their suspicions, that a professed Catholic cannot be an impartial translator of the Scriptures. At this I am not astonished. I know many Catholics, who entertain suspicions equally unfavourable with regard to Protestants: and perhaps there are few, on either side, who are entirely divested of such prejudices. I have professed no more, in that respect, than what, I trust, I shall be able to perform; only let not my cause be prejudged.

Another gentleman, who assumes the name of *Origen*, is afraid that I am about to sacrifice the interests of Mother Church, by exposing the faults of a version which she holds in such high estimation, and which the Council of Trent has declared to be authentic Scripture. To this I answer, that as I will by no means affect to conceal the faults of the *Vulgate*, so neither will I affect to expose them. I will give the best translation I can of what I take to be the most genuine copy of the originals, without minding how much it may differ from any version whatsoever. If this, and what I have said in my *Prospectus*, p. 104, be not sufficient to allay *Origen's* fears, I must leave them to be dispelled by time and re-consideration.

To the writer of a card, recommending the perusal of Wakefield's *Enquiry*, I have to say, that I have carefully perused it; and that the pleasure I received from that perusal would have been much greater, if the author had enforced his favourite system with less violence.

From several persons I have received advices about the œconomy of my work. One counsels me to make my version as strictly literal as possible; another, to make it perfectly free. The former says I should retain all the Hebraisms, however uncouth and obscure they may seem; the latter is for retaining not one of them. It would be impossible for me to follow both these counsels, and therefore I shall follow neither.

A Northumberland correspondent hopes I will not omit to insert Canne's marginal references. This I can by no means comply with : a great number of Canne's references are chimerical, and serve only to crowd the page, and bewilder the reader. But I will insert such references, as I think real and useful ones; and consequently retain the greater part of those that are in the margins of the best editions of our present public version.

I am asked by *Philobiblos*, if I mean not to give a small edition without the critical notes, for the use of those who may not be able to purchase the large one? Alas! I know not yet what encouragement I may have to give ONE edition. When I shall have published my *Proposals* (which will be next winter) and seen how they are relished, it will then be time enough to think of extending my plan.

The Critical Reviewers (Jan. 1787) may indeed "rest secure," that as little deviation as possible will be made from the language of the present version; to which, in fact, my translation, at every new touch, more and more approximates.

In setting about to transcribe my MS. for the press, I find some difficulty in fixing upon the most proper distribution of the page; and should be glad to have the opinion of the learned on that head. For example, should the various readings and renderings be separated from the explana-

tory

tory notes, or mixed with them in the order in which they occur? Should either, or both, be printed in columns? Should every note begin a new line for the fake of diftinction; or be feparated only by a dafh for the fake of fparing paper?

Some of my learned friends are for having the explanatory notes only at the bottom of the page; and for throwing all the reft among the critical remarks; leaving only in the text the refpective fymbols of addition, fubtraction, correction, or variation. This would certainly fave me a great deal of labour; but would not, I fear, be fo fatisfactory to the reader. When we fee a referential mark in the text of a work, we are glad to find the reference as readily as poffible; and naturally look for it on the fame page. I am therefore apt to think, that moft readers will be pleafed with a diftribution that fpares them the trouble of conftantly turning to the end of a volume, to feek in a large field of critical difcuffion, what they wifh to fee at one glance.

Few are capable of weighing the motives and examining the foundations on which a correction of the prefent text has been made; or why fuch a reading has been preferred by the tranflator to fuch another reading: but almoft all are capable of underftanding, and have a right to know, that fuch a correction, and fuch a reading, are made on fuch and fuch authorities.

Such, at leaft, is the light I view things in; by putting myfelf in the fituation of thofe who are not acquainted with the learned languages; but who yet make a ferious ftudy of the Scriptures, and are defirous of knowing the real ftate in which they have been handed down to us.

Let me, once more, intreat thofe gentlemen who have by them any remarks on particular paffages (which they mean not, themfelves, to publifh) to be fo kind as to communicate them. They fhall be thankfully received, and fairly acknowledged.

F I N I S.

www.ingramcontent.com/pod-product-compliance
Lightning Source LLC
Chambersburg PA
CBHW020256090426
42735CB00009B/1108